Mister Lucky

The lucky escapes and coincidences that
helped me through hardships, and the war,
to a long and happy innings.

by

Ivan V.L. Potter

with Hugh Frostick

First published in the United Kingdom in 2017 by
Frostick Publishing
17 Meadow Close, Great Bromley, Colchester CO7 7UG
www.frostick.co.uk
ISBN: 978-0-9957938-1-1

Typeset by Frostick Publishing, Great Bromley
Printed and bound by CZ Design & Print,
Bishops Stortford 01279 657769

Contents

Foreword

Ivan was born between the wars, a true son of the Suffolk soil where he was brought up learning all the secrets of the countryside.

With the outbreak of the Second World War Ivan became a member of the local Home Guard. Later he found himself a member of a clandestine "Stay behind" party intent on impeding any invasion force.

In 1943 Ivan volunteered for Flying Duties in the Royal Air Force and trained up as Wireless Operator/Air Gunner on heavy bombers. At the end of hostilities and after his demob, Ivan joined British Railways. He worked his way up from track laying to being a guard, and had many years travelling around East Anglia with numerous escapades along the way.

In 1983 Ivan was a founder member of the Aircrew Association in Suffolk, and became our Branch Treasurer for many years.

I have greatly enjoyed sharing stories of the old days and the war with Ivan and other Association members over the years, and I am delighted that he has managed to get his stories into print to reach a wider audience.

Best of luck, Mr. Lucky!

Jim Betteridge
Suffolk Air Crew Association

Preface
An introduction to Mister Lucky

I wanted to share some stories from my eventful life. As I wrote some notes about it, I realised how lucky I had been with near misses, where I could have quite easily been badly maimed or killed. I have often considered myself to be Mr. Lucky and, as I jotted down the incidents and saw how many of them there were, I decided on that for the title of my book.

For each of my lucky incidents we have depicted a four-leaved clover in the text like this 🍀. (I have had some bad luck as well, of course, but I don't feel the need to dwell on those times!)

I am grateful to my friend Jim Betteridge, a long time Secretary of Suffolk & District Air Crew Association, for writing my foreword. Jim was a pilot on the Berlin airlifts, and became an instructor on Avro Shackletons. He would have made Squadron Leader if he hadn't thumped some bloke in Australia! He is just one of many wonderful friends I made in the ACA.

I thank Mr. and Mrs. Samuels, the owners of The Wellington at Feltwell, Norfolk, for allowing me to reproduce a part of their tribute mural on my book cover. I also thank the artist, Colin Mason, for his permission, and for creating such beautiful artwork that I wanted it on my book! I was honoured to be invited to help unveil it this year.

I dedicate this book of my life story to my daughter Sonia, my late wife Sally who kept me going for 53 years, and my lady friend Joy who has kept me going for the past 7 years.

I hope you enjoy reading my stories.

Ivan V.L. Potter
Ipswich, October 2017

Chapter 1
Some family background

I was born in 1924 in South-East Suffolk. My father was Othneil Samuel Charles Potter, from Baylham. Not surprisingly, with a moniker like that which was often misspelled, Dad was known as Charlie. Why his parents gave him such an unusual Egyptian name, meaning Lion of God or something, we don't know!

My mother, Christina Vera Whinney (known as Vere), was from Stutton where her parents kept a small holding at the house and grounds of Stutton Tidal Mill on the River Stour, opposite Mistley.

Stutton tidal mill, mother lived in the house shown on the right

Dad was born in 1903 at Baylham, but at some point the family moved to Wherstead. He worked on the farm at Pannington Hall (now known as Jimmy's Farm) with his girlfriend called Margaret Klein. Her father was a German shepherd (no, not a dog) who came over long before the Great War and married an Englishwoman from up north. They had a rough time of it during the First World War. The police had to guard their house for a while, because some people from Ipswich wanted to come out and kill him!

Dad moved to London as a probationary policeman in the Metropolitan Police. He got booted out, however, as on a weekend at home he had a liaison with my mother. Getting my fifteen-year-old mother pregnant did not go down too well with the police. Not only was that a crime, but also the constables were not allowed to marry without proper permissions from above. So, Dad had to leave the force and went back to Suffolk farming.

My mother was born in 1908. Her parents, William and Georgiana Kate Whinney (known as Kate) lived at Hubbard's Hall in Bentley by

that time, not far away. They rented the house along with 120 acres of farm land from Lord Tollemache, of the brewing family in Tolly Cobbold. Mother had a little Shetland pony and trap to deliver the milk down to Stutton village, when she lived at home. In the Great War she said she saw the Zeppelin get shot down somewhere over Colchester that eventually crashed at Billericay.

Dad came back to live with Mum in a part of the farmhouse next to her parents, and started working on the farm at that time. They got married on Valentine's Day 1924, meaning I was born at Hubbard's Hall just nine days the right side of the blanket.

I was named Ivan Victor Llewellyn Potter. My birthday was February 23rd, which was Russian Army Day, and that's why they called me Ivan! I am not sure where the Victor came from – no one had any idea why, when I asked. There were no other Victors in the family that I know of, but maybe it was because we had recently won the Great War.

It was my maternal Grandmother's idea to call me Llewellyn, which comes from a Welsh legend she liked from Beddgelert near Snowden. The Prince Llewellyn had a hound called Gelert that used to guard his baby son when he went out. One day the prince returned and saw his son was missing. When his dog came in, covered in blood, the prince assumed the dog had attacked the child. He killed his hound, before he heard the baby crying under the cradle. When he found a dead mountain lion nearby, he realised that his faithful hound had actually saved the baby. My mother's sister, Uncle Harold, had been given the same middle name before me.

So, my full name is quite a mouthful, and my two younger brothers didn't get off much lighter than me.

Ian Stanley Edwin Potter (known as Stan) was 10 years younger than me and Michael John Charles Potter (known as Mick) was 15 years younger. (There was also a still-born sister at some point, who was not named. That was a thing you never spoke about in those days, but our mother let it out one day when someone asked about just having boys in the family.)

Dad asked Mum, "Why do you want to lumber them with three forenames? They will only use one in their life!"

Another time, at the Registrar's Office for Michael, he said to her, "You crucify them boys, giving them all those names. They have the length of the alphabet to do each time they write out their full name!"

Dad was over six feet tall, weighed seventeen stone, and when I was twelve years old he could put me on one hand, my mother on the other, where he could raise us both up off the ground on either side. He could pick up a coomb of corn, a sack that weighed about the same as him, just with his teeth! He was a wonderful father and the nicest chap you could ever meet. He was well educated but very countrified in many ways and always held a strong Suffolk accent. He never, ever swore at all. The worst we ever heard was maybe a "Damn!" if he was severely annoyed.

He was a fine horseman, becoming head horseman and foreman at Pannington Hall throughout the war, and stayed there until the early fifties. We boys all adored him and agreed he was the greatest man that ever lived.

The same could not be said of my mother, from my point of view. She had some admirable talents and was a real tough nut. She could easily harness a horse and do the harrowing. She had a .410 shotgun of her own but could shoot any gun, even a 12 bore, and not so many women would do that in those days. She once blew some boyfriend's window in with a shotgun, we were told!

Mum said this coypu had it coming!

4

As far I was concerned, at times she was the cruellest women that ever walked the earth. She would often knock us boys over. I can remember her sitting on my shoulders to keep me down while she beat my backside with a hand brush. Our Grandmother once threatened to call the police on her own daughter.

Mum with her satchel for the money on her milk round, pictured outside Hubbard's Hall

I used to collect swords, cutlasses and rapiers before I went in the RAF. One day, Stan had been play-fighting with a friend, using two swords in the main living room and they had nicked a big gash along the back of the settee. Unfortunately, it had just been beautifully reupholstered and had looked like new! They covered up the damage with cushions but when Mum came home, she soon found out. The other boy had left by then so, as well as Stan, she set about the innocent Michael with a cane, assuming he must be guilty too.

She had an indoor broom, a thick cane with a small brush on the end to reach the cobwebs up high, and very whippy it was, too. The dog was playing up and was about to cop a whack, and Mick wanted to protect it. He was sitting in the chair and reached down to grab the dog, and in doing so he got the broom head right on the nut. It knocked him senseless for a time, with blood trickling down.

After I had moved away, their milk was left in the cans two fields away. Stan had not collected the milk on the way home from school one day when it was his turn. Mum shouted at him, "Go and get the milk!" Stan rebelled, saying "I'm not going!" She said, "Oh yes you are!" And she beat him with a stick across the fields, and any time that he stopped she would hit him again. He picked up the cans and came home, and she said, "I told you that you would get the milk!" He laughed and said, "I don't care! You had to come with me!" at which point she whacked him again! Stan was as tough as she was.

5

Mum loved all the men, and a man could do nothing wrong in her eyes, except us boys, apparently, whom she thrashed! I don't know what Dad thought about Mum beating us. I suppose most of the time he was not there to see it. We boys just had to put up with it. He copped it too, at times. She stabbed him in the back with a carving knife when she was angry, but didn't cause any major damage.

I do have some fond memories of her, of course, as there were good times when she was in a fine mood, but I didn't really love her, and don't know why she behaved like that.

My mother had a sister Phyllis and a brother Harold. Aunt Phyllis married a farm worker called Bill Munson from Wherstead; they lived in Belstead, and she died in her sixties. They never had children and I did not have much contact with them, except I remember she kept a pig on her allotment at the beginning of the war, and fed it on any scraps she could find from the village. When the time came to kill it, she was terribly upset as she had raised it from a piglet. She shared the meat around the family for which we were very grateful.

Uncle Harold Llewellyn Whinney was a slight fellow who died aged only 21, when I was about 7 years old. He was working in the fields when the trace horse, the leading one of the pair, swung round suddenly and the chain whacked Harold in the back, which caused a large lump to develop. It didn't hurt that much and didn't really bother him.

Harold with the horses

6

Some months later, however, Harold caught pneumonia and was admitted to hospital. The doctor saw the lump and thought it was something to do with the pneumonia. He operated on it, without permission, and paralysed Harold who died four months later.

After that, every Sunday, Grandmother would play the song "Will the angels play their harps for me" on a 78 r.p.m. record. His death broke her heart.

Uncle Harold with his parents, William and Kate Whinney

I don't know too much about Dad's side of the family. We didn't see much of our relatives as everyone was always working so hard. They might just meet up with us at Christmas or a birthday.

His father was the master blacksmith at Baylham. His mother was a school teacher, and she finished up teaching at Wherstead, the village next to Belstead. After my grandfather Potter was killed in the Great War, she remarried the verger of All Saints Church, Ipswich, so I had a step-grandad called Stanley Newman. I remember pulling the rope to ring the single bell for one of his services at All Saints when I was ten years old. He already had a son and daughter but I have no idea what happened to their mother.

Dad was the second of five children. Aunt Nellie was a couple of years older and moved to London, so we rarely saw her. Uncle Stan became the station sergeant at Hounslow Police Station in the Metropolitan Police, and he plays a big part in my story later on. Auntie Dorothy married Jack Lambert, a nurse porter at Ipswich hospital. and they lived in Bent Lane, Kesgrave. Uncle Laurie worked for Ransomes, Sims & Jefferies who made ploughs and lawnmowers in Ipswich.

Aunt Nell, Charles (my Dad), Uncle Stan, Great uncle Sam, Aunt Dorothy and Margaret Klein. In front are Uncle Laurie and Margaret's daughter, Claire

Dad's uncle Samuel Potter remained at Baylham. I only found out in recent years, from a chap giving a talk at Martlesham Heath Aviation Society, that he had won a Conspicuous Gallantry medal in WW1. He came out of the army and became a police sergeant in

8

Ipswich, and that's probably why Dad and Uncle Stan decided to join the police.

Uncle Harold, Granny Kate, Grandad William, Charlie (Dad),
Aunt Phyllis, myself (almost too short to get in the photo) & Mum

The two Newman children, Dad's half-brother and sister, were Edwin (Ted) and Barbara.

Ted was in the Royal Artillery during the war in a searchlight and anti-aircraft team stationed out on concrete forts in the water near the Isle of Wight. More about Ted later.

Barbara was a gorgeous lady and a lovely Aunty. She looked like a model and married Tom Fleming from East London. Uncle Tom was a club singer, who performed with Geraldo and his Orchestra, but his main job was as an ink maker. He had to make a tankful of ink every day for the printing works.

Uncle Ted

9

They lived in Plaistow and knew the Kray Twins quite well. Tom told a tale about how he was in their favourite pub nicknamed the Glory Hole. One of the brothers said, "Give us your house key for a while." You didn't say no to them. A while later, the Kray came back and said, "Don't go in your front room for a couple of days, it is full of whisky. One case will be left for you." Tom loved a drink. A little while later, he was asked "Have you tried that whisky, yet?" He said he hadn't got onto it yet. "Well, don't bother, it is no good, so just tip it way. That geezer won't be supplying us anymore. He's helping prop up the A13."

I got quite close to the Flemings when they moved to Ipswich in their retirement years. They looked after our home and dogs when we went on holiday to the USA. Old habits die hard; when I said I needed to buy a couple of shirts one day, Tom asked "Don't things just fall off a lorry, here? You can get anything in the East End!"

Tom's was with the Chindits out in Burma during the war and was greatly aided by the Gurkhas. He said they saved his life in the jungle several times, but he wouldn't really talk about it. If snakes came on the television at any time he would immediately get up and walk out of the room. Uncle Tom and Aunty Barbara left me a decent sum of money when they died, so I thought I would use it to support the Gurkhas, which I still do every year in memory of them.

Sadly, I have no decent picture of Tom and Barbara. Here is Tom entertaining my dog whilst he was dog sitting for us in his latter years

Chapter 2
Childhood on the farm

A s was usual in those days, when Dad got new work he had to find different accommodation. As we moved around so much, I attended several different schools.

I started out living at Hubbard's Hall with Grandparents Whinney. When I was about four years old, Dad got a job at Hart's Farm in Wherstead. We moved to a farm cottage opposite The Ostrich Inn (now known as the Oyster Reach) at the bottom of Bourn Hill. When I was five he moved us to Mann's Farm in Holbrook. It was at that time that the Royal Hospital School was being built, so Dad applied for a job as labourer. He worked there for about four years but, in doing so, we had to vacate our house at the farm. We moved to a small cottage back in Belstead, which we called The Little House, not far from Charity Cottage where they lived later. We lived on the one storey side, with only two rooms and a kitchen, and Bill Meadows lived next door in the two storey side.

Mum and Dad at the Little House

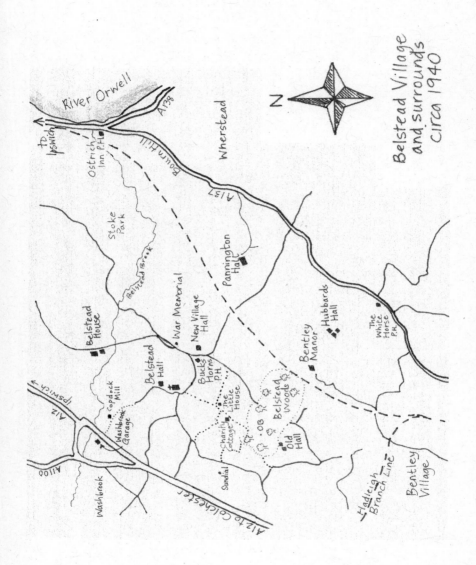

River Orwell

A139

to Ipswich

Ostrich Inn P.H.

Bourn Hill

A137

Wherstead

Stoke Park

Belstead Brook

Pannington Hall

War Memorial

New Village Hall

Belstead House

Copdock Mill

Belstead Hall

Washbrook Garage

Bucks Horns P.H.

Charity Cottage

The Little House

Sandial

OB

Belstead Woods

Belstead Old Hall

Bentley Manor

Hubbards Hall

The White Horse P.H.

A12 to Ipswich

A1100

Washbrook

A12 to Colchester

Hadleigh Branch Line

Bentley Village

N

Belstead Village and surrounds circa 1940

12

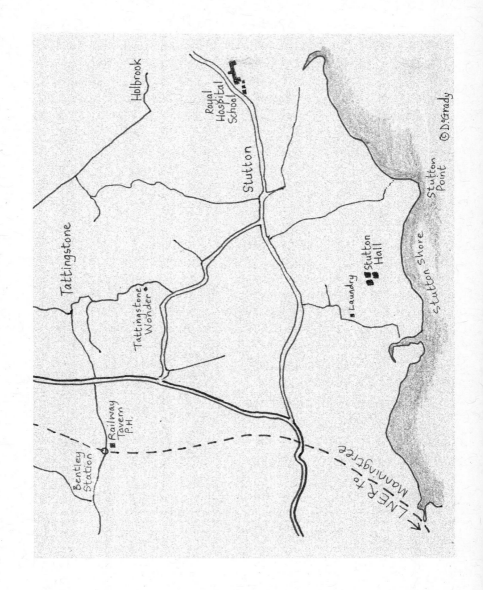

Holbrook

Royal Hospital School

Stutton

Stutton Point

© D.ᵉGrady

Tattingstone

Stutton Hall

Laundry

Stutton Shore

Tattingstone Wonder

Railway Tavern P.H.

Bentley Station

LNER to Manningtree

13

Belstead was a typical rural village, with farm houses and cottages dotted here and there, a school, church and chapel, a pub and a couple of big manor houses. The main part of Belstead is centred in a little triangle comprising the chapel, school, and the war memorial at the southern end. To the north is Holly Lane, where Stan lived for a time. St Mary's church and Belstead Hall is off to the west of the centre towards Copdock and not far from their church. (The Copdock Rectory was built right next door to the Belstead Rectory.) The road to church went down south of the triangle, then turned into Buck's Horns Lane past The Buck's Horns Pub. On the way along that lane, nearing the church, Little House and Charity Cottage both lay off a farm track leading south to Bentley Old Hall. This old house was situated on the edges of what was known as Baldrough's Wood, but known in recent years as Belstead or Bentley Woods, depending on the direction from which you walked into them!

Charity Cottage was a thatched cottage built in the 1500s. It was originally called Crope Hall. Apparently, the rent from this dwelling went towards a coal charity, so that everyone in the village got a free hundredweight of coal for their fire every year. Hence, it became known as Charity Cottage and it had been renamed that before Mum and Dad moved the hundred yards to it from the Little House in 1938. The cottage was later bought by and is still in the family, although now with a tiled roof to replace the thatch.

The field opposite the cottage is said to be the highest spot in Suffolk. They wanted to build a new airfield there at one time, causing a lot of opposition and marches by locals all around, but it never happened.

Young Stan, myself, Mother, Molly (can't remember who she was) and Father at Charity Cottage in the late 1930s

After the building work finished at Holbrook School, Dad went to work for Cubitt & Gotts, the Ipswich building firm. He stayed there until the beginning of the war and then went back to farming for the Wilson brothers at Pannington Hall, Wherstead, as did Mum. Dad did every job there was to do on the farm and was the head horseman. He was a good thatcher and I remember in September 1939, when he had twelve corn stacks to thatch, how much I enjoyed helping him after I left off work.

Dad and the cows at Hart's Farm on Bourn Hill

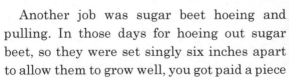

Another job was sugar beet hoeing and pulling. In those days for hoeing out sugar beet, so they were set singly six inches apart to allow them to grow well, you got paid a piece work rate of one shilling and a penny (1s 1d) per hundred yards. Once you got the knack of it you could make good money. These days, the seeds are sown singly so there is no need to thin them out.

When Dad and Mum were working on the farm, Stan and I helped in our spare time as soon as we were old enough. In those days life was hard and everyone had to work. We all worked very long hours at times but it helped make us a good living.

Three weeks after I was born, I had what I count as my first lucky escape whilst my parents were drilling corn. My father was driving the drill across the field behind the two horses. Mother used to ride on the back to make sure the corn was running properly through the drill, so I was wrapped up in a blanket inside a tin bath wedged at the front. The drill was towed along on a wooden beam, with the steering piece having two small wheels.

When they got to the end of the row, a pheasant flew out of the hedge. That spooked the horses and they whipped round, tilting the beam enough to throw the bath off with me in it, and I landed in front of the oncoming prongs. Luckily, Dad managed to halt the horses before I was run over in my blanket. I was picked up and dusted down, none the worse for my ordeal. ❧

At Hubbard's Hall, one of my earliest memories, and the first job I remember doing, was stone picking to improve the tilth. I was four years old and I would pick up the bigger ones that would interfere with the agricultural machinery and put them in buckets which I couldn't possibly lift. The men would cart them away to fill in holes around the farm tracks and lanes where the puddles formed. I well remember how my back felt after a few hours of that toil.

Another early memory was the butcher, Mr Bullard from Tattingstone, coming to slaughter the pigs at the farm. He took the intestines out and washed them out for use as sausage skins which was a very strange sight.

One of the cart horses we had was called Smiler. From when I was four years old, Dad brought him home of an evening and, after taking all the harness off Smiler, he set me on his back. I would hold onto his mane to ride bareback the 50 yards down the lane to their meadow. I could open the gate and let him through, with the other horse following. One day, before we got to the gate, Smiler decided he must have a drink in the pond when I wasn't expecting it. He stooped his neck down and shot me over his neck. I somersaulted to land feet first in the pond. I yelled out in surprise and Smiler took off back to the farm. My parents came running to see why Smiler had come back alone and found me stuck up to my waist in mud. If I had gone in head first, that would have been me well done for. ❁

We all had shot guns on the farm. I had a number 1 shot gun (about the same size as a .22) from a young age. From the age of five I used that gun to scare linnets off the mustard seed. I wasn't strong enough to cock it myself by hand, so I used to rest the barrel on the end of my shoe while I cocked the stiff hammer. One time I managed to pull the trigger at the same time and put a hole in my shoe. I only lost a bit of my big toe and the nail still shows it now. ❁ I screamed and ran home for my mother to bandage it. Mum was not so concerned about my missing body parts as the need for a major shoe repair!

Granny Kate used to go to Ipswich in her pony and cart every Saturday. I would go with her sometimes and we would leave our cart in the back of the Bell Pub at the end of Wherstead road, this side of Stoke Bridge. The busy Cattle Market off Handford Road was always full of excitement. I remember the men holding up a big hand of bananas, 20 or 30 of them, and people were bidding for them at 2d or 3d each.

There was one incident coming back on the cart by the Ostrich Inn. The road used to go straight up through Wherstead on to Hubbard's Hall. We were stopped at the bottom by police, at Hart's farm on the left of Bourn Hill. They told us a petrol tanker had been going up the hill when the driver missed a gear. The lorry ran back into the bank where the collision had fractured the tank, and petrol was leaking out and running down the road. They made us pull in and put sacking on the horses' hooves to stop the metal from making sparks that might risk setting it alight.

When Grandfather went to market he would call in the Ostrich Inn quite a bit, as Grandmother considered beer to be a most dreaded thing in life. She hated it. He would call in there for a few pints and the horse would steer him home. Kate gave him a right earful when he got back, but at least he got his beer.

I was very close to my Granny Kate, who I thought a wonderful lady. She kept two cows and delivered the milk in cans to Tattingstone village. She would carry a three-gallon can on either side of her and ladle it out into women's jugs and churns by the door.

When I was old enough I would go with her on Saturday to deliver eggs and the butter she made. We delivered to the Tattingstone White Horse, which was produce just for their own use, as pubs never did food back then.

The Landlord of the White Horse was Tom Woolard, and this was his very first photograph that mother took

For someone's birthday, Kate would design the butter into the shape of a nest with bird's eggs in it. She was very clever like that. My brother still has her butter pat and the hand churn she made the butter with, and the purchase bill for £3.

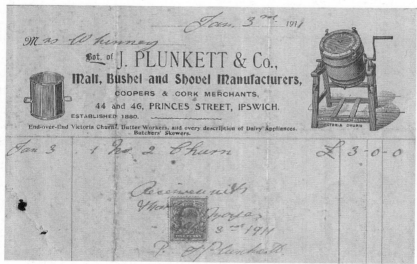

On Saturday mornings I often went to help the village blacksmith. Mr. George Ward taught me how to make horseshoes and chains. One of the best jobs was helping with the shoeing of cartwheels which were made by the Southgate brothers in their workshop nearby. My job was to fill cans of water to quench the red-hot steel rims that had been placed around the wooden wheels, so as to shrink them tightly into place.

During summer months when the corn was being cut we would go into the harvest fields and catch rabbits that were hiding in the corn. When they broke cover, we would chase them and try to knock them over with our sticks. This was great fun and if we caught more than the family could eat, we could take them into Ipswich and sell them for about sixpence each to the butcher. Some of that we had for pocket money and some would go into housekeeping for our boots and clothes.

In the winter months, when the corn stacks were being threshed, we would watch for the mice and rats running out of the stacks and kill them with our sticks.

Another winter job was to clear ditches and layer the hedges. We made use of any suitable wood for logs, linen props and pea sticks. I had great fun as I was put in charge of the bonfire, burning up all the rubbish. Afterwards, I'd carry away the biggest pole I could manage, whilst Dad would carry a good armful.

A favourite pastime was babbing for eels at Belstead Brook. I had a schoolboy's stick and line, with coarse, worsted wool tied on the end, and would thread a worm onto that. I cast it in and when an eel grabbed it, the wool caught on his teeth and I could flick him out, 18 to 24 inches long. I took them home for eating.

We all loved going down to Stutton Shore on the North bank of the River Stour. When Dad's aunts came down from London, we took a horse and a cart and went all the way down there past Fison's Manor. (This was Stutton Hall, but a top man from Fisons  fertilisers lived there.) It was a big place with lots of servants.

Old postcard of Stutton

Granny's two sisters, with the maiden name of White, lived in a pair of cottages not far from Stutton Village Hall. Their husbands worked on the manor. In their garden they had a special brick-built laundry room where they did all the laundry for the manor. It had a

19

copper in each of the four corners, a big old-fashioned stove that stood in the middle to heat up all the smoothing irons, and tables all around the walls for doing the ironing.

After the war we were only able to bike down to the shore as the gates were locked to keep the cows in. We would take everything with us and cook the meals on a campfire on the beach. I don't ever remember Dad coming down with us. He was always busy doing some job, and we'd go and help him when we wanted to spend time with him, as he never played any sports or games with us.

Lower Street in Stutton, from an old postcard

Chapter 3
School days

I started school in January when I was nearly five. My first school was Holbrook Infant School. We had to walk across two fields, I suppose with my mother, but I can't remember doing it. I was not very long there, less than a year, and I don't recall the teachers.

I do remember I teased the girls when I saw they could not keep the stitches on their needles. The teacher told me off and said, "If you keep laughing at them you will have to sit with the girls and do knitting!" I had been taught knitting, sewing and crochet by Grandmother Kate, so I could already knit better than many of them and the teacher got shot down in flames.

Next, I went to Belstead school, which was only for infants. The school teacher was a Mrs Jennings. I didn't get into much trouble at school, that I remember, but we had pail lavatories and they were taken out from a hatch at the back for emptying. We boys used to open the hatch when the girls were on the toilet to tickle their bottoms with stinging nettles!

At that time my Dad was doing a six-mile bicycle ride to Holbrook from Belstead, six days a week in all weathers, for a wage of thirty-two shillings a week. His wages as a farm labourer were 27s a week, but doing labouring he could get between 32s and 35s. That was not far to cycle for those days but not much fun after a hard day's labouring.

One day I decided to go after school to meet him coming home from work. I had no working bicycle of my own at that time, so I took my mother's old-fashioned one. It was so high for me that sitting on the seat was impossible; I had to stand on the pedals and reach the handlebars above my head. As I was riding through the village my feet must have slipped off the pedals, causing me to fall and I hit myself hard on the lower crossbar of the frame. My father came along and found me in a pool of blood and he carried me home. Mother went to Copdock to fetch Mrs Everett, our district nurse, who put seven stitches in the wound in my scrotum. I had badly crushed my right testicle which has never grown since. From then on, the boys at school used to call me One Hung Low or Ivan Bollockoff!

Some people might not count this painful event as being very lucky. I call it a lucky escape, seeing as I was still able to use my remaining equipment and reproduce! ✿

This is Stan and young Mick on mother's bicycle upon which I had my injury. Like me before him, Stan could nowhere near reach the pedals from the seat!

It seems in those days I was a bit prone to accidents on bicycles as I crashed the same bike going down Prettyman's Hill in Belstead, causing a nasty cut on my head. I also have a little scar near my eye from when I was biking home with mother from the Chelmondiston Show. A bat flew into my face and snagged me with its claw.

From Belstead school, the children went on to a senior school, either Wherstead, Copdock & Washbrook or Ipswich, depending on where you lived in our scattered village. My school was Copdock where they had Mrs Stocks as junior teacher, a different Mrs Jennings taught the infants, and the seniors were taught by the marvellous headmistress, Mrs Dunnett. She ruled the school with a rod of iron and took no nonsense from anyone. She knew everything, it seemed. She took us boys for cricket and football and was a very fair referee and a good umpire.

She lost her husband during the First World War. She would get us to fold up newspapers to make sticks to light the school fires with, telling us that was what the men started fires with in the trenches. Fold them over and over to make solid sticks to get the fire going. She used to bring in papers and we would fold them up for use at school and for her own fire at home.

Every country school had a garden to plant vegetables. Mrs Dunnet showed us how to do that, and I think the produce helped her to keep going. There was a little wooden sweet shop opposite the school run by Miss Sumpton. When her brother came up from London he used to grab handfuls of sweets and throw them over to us children in the playground, so he was a very popular chap!

The day that brother Stan was born, 3rd of December, I was sent on a bike to fetch Mrs Everett to come and help my mother, who was having the birth at home. With all that palaver I was late to school and as I went rushing through the gates I snagged and tore my short trousers at the back.

I had to knock on the school door to come in, as school had already started, and then had to stand in front of Mrs Dunnett to explain. All the kids could see my predicament and were laughing like mad. She asked them why they were laughing, and someone said "Ma'am, he's got his trousers all torn." I explained what had happened. She told me to go with another boy to the toilets, take the shorts off, and he would bring them back to her. Then she asked one of the girls, Francis Rush, to mend my trousers, and half an hour later they were brought back to me to wear so I could join the class. (I didn't get a pair of long trousers until I started work!)

I never had any homework to do, as it was not the thing in those days, but I know my schooling gave me a good training for my future.

Mrs Dunnett was quite some teacher. She was greatly respected and made many a man, in my opinion. When a retirement party was thrown for her, there were so many people turned up to thank her that the Village Hall was full up and a very large number had to stay outside.

Just before I left school, there were quite a few major events in my life. My Uncle Harold had died, leaving no son on the farm. Just four months after that, Grandfather William died from cancer. He was

23

transported on a cart from the farm to the churchyard which shows on his funeral bill.

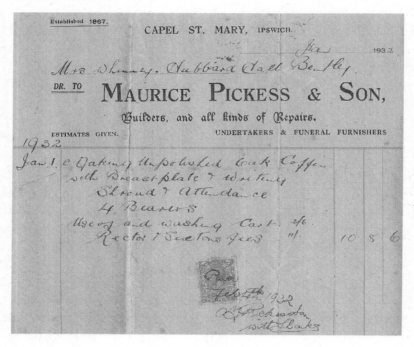

Granny tried to run the farm herself with two live-in men who came to work for her. I used to stay at the farm most weekends to help her as well. She had a sixteen-year-old Barnardo's girl to help around the house and I slept in the same room as her. It was to her that I lost my virginity at the age of thirteen.

I think the men must have been lazy and did not do the work properly, as my grandmother eventually decided she had to give up the farm. She held a farm sale to sell the farm implements and everything. It raised her £52-12-6 but she had almost nothing left after she had paid Cranfield the miller, the bull man for servicing the cows, and her other creditors.

Chapter 4
Helping Gran to make ends meet

J ust after the Christmas holiday I left school, a little bit early. I would be fourteen in the February but I imagine they said something like, "There is no point Ivan coming in for six more weeks as he's learned sod all whilst he has been here, and a bit more time won't make any difference!"

I started work and left home, simply because I moved in with my widowed grandmother Kate Whinney, both to help her and to keep her company.

She had moved into Bentley Old Hall, built in the 1500s, about a mile from Mum and Dad's house. The land had been given to Admiral Tollemache and apparently the wood the house was made from came from some of his ships. The house had been derelict for ten years at that time but Mr Dunne, who owned the land and house, kindly let Kate move in as she had no money and nowhere else to go. She had no income. Nothing had been paid in, so she got no financial help from the government until she became a pensioner. I don't know why Mr Dunne didn't charge her any rent, but I think as he was the neighbouring farmer, and the house was derelict anyway, he wanted to help her out. He lived in Bentley Hall about a mile and a half away, near Bentley church.

Inside Old Hall

Mr Dunne said he would make the place waterproof, and plough the garden up so she could plant vegetables. He repaired windows and fixed the roof so we didn't need so many buckets around the place. It was a massive job for us to turn over all the flagstones in the main room to make them level, as they were badly worn down by 400 years of footfall.

I helped Granny to manage, but as she could make anything out of nothing, there never seemed to be a problem getting food on the table. There were plenty of rabbits and we grew our own vegetables.

She and Mum used to pick wild primroses and violets to bunch up, and then she'd cycle to town on Tuesdays and Fridays to sell them in the Stoke area of Ipswich. A bunch of primroses was tuppence, or they fetched thruppence with a centre of violets.

Rabbits were sold for about nine pence or a shilling each. Those that were not sold privately were bought by Mr. "Porky" Prior who had a butcher's shop on Wherstead Road. I think he had a soft spot for Gran as we always seemed to have a good piece of meat to cook for the weekend.

We used to catch pheasants very secretly without a gun, using an old gypsy way of catching them. We'd get dried peas, soak them and thread them on horse hair an inch a part, then put them in the oven to dry. We'd then cut the hair to leave a quarter of an inch sticking out each side. These would be scattered in with ordinary peas where the birds feed after coming out of the woods in the morning. The pheasants would eat one of these hairy ones and get it stuck in their crop. That would stop them flying off and while they were worrying about that we would hit them on the head with a ten-foot stick.

Another way to get them was with luminous snares from Youngs of Sheffield, set on the end of twelve-foot hazelnut poles. When you shine up your light onto the birds faces at night they won't fly, as they can't see where to go. You could slip the snare over and sharply yank it down. I would come home from work and Gran might say, "They are roosting tonight in the hazel wood!" and we could go in and find them. We had to do this poaching to get enough money and food to live on.

Mother used to catch moles, and would skin them and stretch and nail the skins on the old corn barn door at Hubbard's Hall, with the fur next to the wood to allow the inner side to dry out. She would parcel them up and send them to Youngs of Sheffield and get paid fourpence a skin.

The picture shows those barn doors, and my Fairy cycle, which was my first two-wheeled bike when I was aged about 4 or 5.

We would glean from the fields as much as possible. The farmer would sometimes leave a "policeman", being a shock of corn, which meant you were not allowed to glean from that field. It indicated the farmer had not yet been round with the horse-drawn rake. They didn't always rake up, but if the crop was very ripe the ears would fall off during harvest and many would be lost, so they would try to recover it. We spent hours and hours bending our backs on the fields.

The gleaned corn we would thresh ourselves, rubbing it by hand. We took about 14lbs at a time down to Thurman's Flour Mill near the Bell at Ipswich, and he would mix that in with his and give us some flour back. Barley and oats we'd gleaned would be kept ourselves for animal feed.

Nancy, Kate's favourite

I stayed with Kate until I went in the Air Force in 1943. I think my parents gave her some money for my upkeep but could not do too much to help her as wages at that time were still very poor and, besides, two more children had arrived in our family. Both Stanley and Michael went to live

27

with Kate at one time or other and remember helping her, very much the same as I had done.

Kate stayed in Old Hall for about twelve years until 1949, when she moved to Thatched Cottages opposite Tattingstone church. She lived on her own in her retirement, but she died not so long after.

I was also earning money by doing other jobs around the area. I did several things for the Wilson family at Belstead Hall, who kept a dairy farm. Mr Wilson was a lovely man, a real gentleman. I would respectfully touch my cap whenever I saw him.

Mr Wilson did weather readings like rainfall and temperatures for the *East Anglian Daily Times.*

Granny Kate at Charity Cottage

There was also a recording sundial, to map the sun strength and so on, using a lens that burned into heat-sensitive paper. This was in a field we all called Sundial Field behind Charity Cottage. When I delivered the milk each day at about half past four, he would give me the new paper. After sunset, I took the old one out to be returned to him, and replaced it with the new one.

One day when I came back from delivering milk to Copdock Rectory, there was such a violent storm that I sheltered under an elm tree. Hailstones came down the size of golf balls. I picked up about half a dozen of these and put them in the empty milk can, then I took them to show him. He laid them out on the table next to a Swan Vestas match, and took a photo of them to print in the *East Anglian.*

Mrs Wilson was lovely too, and she bathed me in cream! I was going into the dairy to collect the milk and cream to deliver, and as I walked up the step Mrs Wilson turned the churn over, but the lid wasn't sealed, so I got completely showered with fresh cream. Flo Pinner used to work in the dairy, and she washed me down and took me home. It took some boiling to get the cream out of my clothes, and they were never quite the same so Mrs Wilson gave Mum 7s and 6d to buy me a new suit.

One evening a week we went to choir practice with Mr Bawd the choirmaster. Afterwards I would go to the barns at Belstead Hall and shoot the rats. I had a fountain pen torch tied to the barrel, so as soon as the light shone on a rat I would fire. All extra earnings!

Mother gathering wild flowers in the woods

Chapter 5
Into long trousers

My first job after leaving school was on a poultry and fruit farm in Copdock. The owner was Mr Frank Plumb, who had a big dent in the side of his jaw where a bullet went in his mouth in the 1914-18 war. He was unmarried, as was his sister who ran the adjacent Post Office.

I got paid 10s and 6d a week, or fifty-two and a half pence in today's money. I gave Granny Kate 5s for housekeeping. (I think my parents topped up Kate with a bit more to help her with my upkeep, just a bob or two.) Half a crown (2s-6d) of my wages went straight to Walton's Cycle shop, where Dad had put down ten shillings deposit on a new bike for me. I had my very own Hopper bicycle with a Sturmey–Archer three gear and a hub dynamo, at just thirteen years old! That was some bike which I kept for about 25 years.

There were various jobs I did for the Post Office and on the farm. Telegrams would come in to the Post Office and, as it was the country postal service, anyone who was available could deliver them. The Plumbs had a whistle to summon me to the Post Office from the farm when a telegram arrived. Later, because of the Air Raid Precautions, they were not allowed to use that, so they had to come and find me. I would just get on my bike and deliver the message, and then wait for a bit in case there was any reply.

The newspapers came on the bus from Ipswich at about twenty past eight in the morning. Not many people took a newspaper in those days so there were just seven for me to deliver, on my new bike, to four big houses in Copdock, and then one each to the policeman, the butcher and harness maker.

One morning in 1937 there had been some very heavy rain which caused some flooding. Whilst out delivering papers, I was about to ride over the Belstead Brook bridge at Washbrook when half of it collapsed in front of me! ♣

I crossed over on the good piece and laid my cycle down in the middle of the road at the other side of the hole, as I knew that a bus would be due shortly. I ran to the grocer's shop just beyond the bridge telling him of the mishap. He said, "Go and tell the policeman, and I will stop the bus!" This was done with all due haste. The next day the newspaper headlines read "Grocer stops bus from crashing into river" with not even a mention of my rather vital involvement!

My main job was looking after two hundred chickens – cleaning sheds, collecting eggs and grading them, and feeding the birds – more or less all on my own. The eggs had to be free of any muck, and some needed to be wiped off with a damp cloth. The cleaner you could keep the nest boxes and perches, the less wiping was needed, of course. I had an egg cup holder fixed onto a scale where I individually weighed every single one of the eggs to put them into three grades: Small were from one and a half ounces, Standard were over two ounces, Large were over two and a half ounces. I packed the graded eggs into large egg crates.

In summer time I had to creosote the sheds. That was some job. I had no protective smock or apron, and in those days if you splashed creosote on your skin it burned like hell. The stuff you buy in the DIY stores today is so weak you can almost bathe in it.

During apple-picking time, after my chicken rounds, I raked up windfalls from around the trees and put them in sacks to go off for cider-making.

I worked for the Plumbs getting on for two years.

*Our neighbour Mr Gladding
with two of his piglets*

Chapter 6
War work at Ransomes & Rapier

T
he war broke out in September 1939. The day after war was declared we found a large number of spent .303 cartridge cases. We had watched the aircraft that fired these rounds, Spitfires and Hurricanes that had taken off from Martlesham airfield near Ipswich. Apparently whilst manoeuvring into formation one of the pilots had his safety button off. He shot down two of his mates, a Spitfire which crashed at Hintlesham killing the pilot, and a Hurricane which came down at Road Farm, Wherstead. My Gran and I went to look at that one and I took Stan on the crossbar of my bike. When we neared the 'plane he caught his foot in the front wheel of my cycle throwing us both over the handlebars onto the road. We both had cuts and bruises and my front wheel was buckled. We collected up a good number of spent bullet cases from the ground, and three of these are now in the Martlesham Heath Control Tower Museum with an account of the incident. I had to carry my cycle home on my shoulder while Gran took Stan home on hers.

A big employer in Ipswich was Ransomes, known for their innovations on ploughs and later with petrol lawnmowers. At that time there were two separate companies, following a split a century before. Ransomes, Sims & Jefferies were still producing agricultural equipment. Ransomes & Rapier were involved in heavy engineering such as for the railways. With the outbreak of war, many factories went over to war work, and Ransomes & Rapier (I shall just refer to it as Ransomes from now on) was no exception.

I went to Ransomes on war work, and found them to be a great firm to work for. There were hundreds of workers at Ransomes so there was a mass of bikes going into the factory with a huge area to park them all. No workers owned cars back then, in general. No one locked up their bike in those days and I never even thought about anyone taking my bike of which I was so proud. A thief would have had plenty to choose from!

I used to cycle in with a chap called King who lived opposite Belstead school. We'd cycle along Belstead Road where every morning there was a nasty little terrier dog that would look out for us and chase us and try to nip at our heels. We got fed up with this, and King said, "I will fix him!" He brought along a bottle of water the next morning, and when the dog came at us he sloshed it out and soaked it. After that, the annoying dog only ever barked from inside his gate.

I was an apprentice plater doing sheet metal and girder work, a job that I really liked. The main things I worked on were mobile cranes, cement mixers, twenty-five pounder gun mountings and aircraft catapults. When I started I was under supervision, until I became a Blue Badge Holder, which meant I could do work on my own without a senior plater supervising. When I turned sixteen I was also able to put in overtime.

When making the chassis for mobile cranes, I would assemble the parts that had been made up, lining up the angles and putting in a bolt every fifth hole. Then the riveters would come and rivet it up.

We made catapults intended for HMS *Apollo*, I think it was. The catapult was a big steel frame with a cable that could shoot a plane into the air from the ship. This was a one-way trip of course, as they couldn't land back onboard a normal ship. They usually used a float plane which would land on the water beside the ship, where it would be picked up by a crane and put back on the catapult and made ready to launch again. We made one of these things and it was shipped out, but when it got to London it was destroyed in a bomb raid, so we had to do it all over again.

The Air Ministry was going mad for cement mixers with all the concrete laying needed for airfields everywhere. There was one tragic accident, where I had seen the bloke being carted off and wondered what had happened. One of the biggest cement mixers had a large drum, similar to those on the lorries today. The ends had to be pressed into shape by cutting a piece of steel, warming it to red heat in the oven, then pressing it to turn the edges up to the required shape. They were trying out a new type of press, but the central pin that lines it up had become stuck and they could not get it out. The furnaceman poured some paraffin on it to soak overnight to help release it. The next morning the first bloke to arrive leaned over and hit it with a hammer. Because it had been beside the furnace the paraffin went off like a gun and the pin flew straight out and passed right through his head and killed him.

We had quite a number of air raids over Ipswich. The town sirens used to go, but it was a big waste of time heading to the air-raid shelter every time that went off, if there were no aircraft causing us a threat. They came up with a system called the cuckoo warning which they only set off if enemy aircraft had been spotted in our vicinity. It went "Woo-hoo Woo-hoo Woo-hoo" and that indicated it was worth stopping work and we would make our way to the shelters.

Mrs Jennings was a middle-aged lady who worked on the 25-ton overhead cranes, about thirty feet up. As soon as the ordinary siren went, she put on her harness, which was attached to a slow-dropping rope. Once the cuckoo warning went, it was my job to dash to wherever the crane was in the workshop and assist her out of the harness when she came down, so we were usually the last two into the shelter.

I worked on a corvette called HMS *Firefly* with my senior plater. We were setting up the degaussing equipment to oppose a magnetic field to deactivate the magnetic mines. We had to thread heavy duty electric cable through 4-inch piping, making up templates to make it fit round the gunwales. At the end of the day, the ship had left the quayside at Ransomes and moved to the main docks, and was moored next to the gasometer overnight.

Early next morning we had just arrived at work when six Focke-Wulf 190s attacked Ipswich Docks and we headed to the shelters. As they came over they were shot at by HMS *Firefly*, and she hit one of them which exploded. We heard that alright from the shelter. When we came out on the all clear signal, we found out what had happened to it. The wings were over by the lock gates. The main fuselage had come to a rapid halt, lodged on Christopherson's dock crane. The aeroplane's engine kept coming for another 50 yards to drop through the roof at Ransomes. It plunged into the floor, right beside my work bench. The pilot carried on another 50 yards and laid mangled up by the steel yard near the swimming pool. That was a day I was very grateful that I went to the shelter! ❧

During this time at Ransomes there were lots of incidents and things to see. We saw the airfield defence guns and a rocket firing system which carried great lengths of cable up into the sky to deter dive-bombers. It was a strange feeling when an air raid was taking place, as shrapnel from the guns at Harwich used to fall all around. When I was cycling through the woods on my way home I could clearly hear it hitting the trees. At night, Gran and I could look out of our windows at Bentley and see the tracer and flak between Harwich and Ipswich.

Butterfly bombs were wicked things. Like a great big cocoa tin, they had wings on the outside and if you touched them they went off. When some of these were dropped over the docks, some workers found one in our yard. They had not seen one before so they took it into the workshop to be examined, where it exploded and killed three of them.

The Hermann was the biggest bomb the Germans dropped on us, and I saw a Hermann being dropped from a Dornier 217. It was apparently aimed for the gasworks but missed by about a quarter of a mile to land in Holywells Park, where it failed to explode. I was with Mop Thomas, the senior plater, hand riveting the staves in a big steel ladder on the long joists outside the girder shop. We heard the noise of the plane and looked up to see it emerge from the clouds at about 500 feet and we saw the bomb drop. We dropped to our hands and knees but it went by us and then of course nothing happened.

The great bomb was defused and dug out, and funnily enough my mate King who I cycled with was operating one of the mobile cranes. They had a job to get it out as it was quite sandy in the park and it kept sinking in whenever they dug around. They put the bomb on display at Cornhill, Ipswich, with a collection bucket for the war effort. That stayed next to Lloyds Avenue for a couple of years.

The bomb dug out of the park – this was given to me unmarked and is of unknown copyright

The army shot down another Dornier that bombed Wattisham and killed a dozen people. We heard the gunfire and we saw the bomber with the smoke pouring out coming down to crash in the top of Gippeswyk Park. Albert Rudland was a friend from school who also worked at Ransomes on a different shift to me. He went and took the two Spandau guns out of the turret and took them home, but the police found out and made him take them back again! The last of the five German crew to bail out landed on the roof of a little cottage in Purplett Street. The Home Guard came along and were very keen to shoot him, but they didn't, and instead they had to fetch a ladder to allow him to get him down.

Albert Rudland later went in the army and became a POW. He was incarcerated with the famous S.O.E. chap, Wing Commander Yeo-Thomas, who escaped several times and there was a book "The White Rabbit" written about his exploits. Albert later told me he sent a letter home to his mother, and in it he put a code "The white rabbit is still alive and kicking." When the book was published, his mother took the letter up to London to show them.

Another mate, Albert Warren from Belstead, was also a POW with him and he eventually got shot by a sniper. I went to see his Dad who showed me his wallet with a bullet hole straight through it.

Funnily enough, working in the factory we realised the Germans are amongst the best engineers in the world. We had a German machine called a nibbler, with a little round steel disk and a knife that went up and down, which could cut quarter-inch steel to shape it. We boys used to cut the metal for chain guards on cranes. After about 1941 there were no more blades available for the machine and it took our lot some weeks to come up with suitable replacement blades that were man enough for the job. I have no problem driving a German car.

Chapter 7
The Home Guard and Secret Army

T he Local Defence Volunteer force was set up after Dunkirk. I reckon most of the village came to our first parade on that sunny Sunday morning at Belstead School. There were maybe thirty of us, mainly men and a few women, with just two old boys carrying the service rifles they brought home from the First World War. The rest of us had shotguns, including my mother with her .410, as nearly everybody in the village had a gun of some sort.

We did parades for a couple of months before the name changed to the Home Guard. I think the farmer in charge of us was called Captain Wilson. The Sergeant was another Great War survivor. All the platoon were from Belstead but, sadly, I can't remember many of their names now.

A month or so after the change of name, in the summer of 1940, a regular army Captain come along to our parade. He said he wanted to form a mobile squad, of six men who must know every house and back door, and every tree and ditch around for miles. I volunteered, along with Laurence Whinney (a relative), George and Fred Ward (brothers, the sons of the local blacksmith who was also called George), Charlie Simpson and George Airey... who had a very nice sister! Those three aforementioned all worked at Belstead Hall. Laurence was the oldest, at 24, and he was made the Sergeant of our patrol. George Ward was the Corporal. I was the youngest of them at just sixteen.

We still stayed with the regular Home Guard, and paraded with them at the same time on a Sunday. After that, the six of us would fall out into the mobile squad, and we would be away and do our own thing. The public story was that if a neighbouring village got into difficulties we could quickly go to help.

Our unit was part of what later became known as Churchill's Secret Army. Units were formed all over the country to become sabotage units to fight behind the Germans if they landed in England. We were given quite a grounding on all aspects of sabotage, away from the regular Home Guard units. We were sworn to secrecy and were not even allowed to tell our families. It was vital that we all had a good knowledge of the local area. Each unit did not know the existence or whereabouts of other units, so that if we were caught we would not be able to tell of their positions.

We had some classroom training from that army Captain. Sometime before Christmas 1942 I was sent to Battle School at Aldeburgh. There, I met Derek Youngs, an old mate from my school who was in another local unit, and we spoke during the course.

The two weeks of high intensive training did not hold back on anything. They really put us through it. We were trained on all sorts of weapons, explosives and booby traps. Simple things, like taking an apple or a swede to push up a vehicle's exhaust, using a stick. Making up wooden wedges with protruding nails, cut with barbs to make them hold in a tyre, to place under a stationary wheel to cause a puncture when the vehicle moved off.

Setting trip wires to trigger nail bombs across the lanes. (For expected motorcycle riders, you put the trip wire a few yards in front of the device so that the flying nails ended up nearer to where the rider would arrive.) We made imitation anti-tank mines, positioned so the tank driver would spot them easily, and in steering to avoid them he would hit the real mines which were well hidden to the side.

There were twelve of us on the course and we were divided into two units, each one with a sergeant in charge. The rivalry was fierce, especially in the unarmed combat bouts. Live ammunition and hand grenades were in regular use. One night we had to make a raid just off the beach towards a farmhouse, a mile over some marshland. We had to crawl on our stomachs, with instructors firing live rounds only two feet above the ground, to give us the feeling of being under enemy fire. The sight of tracer bullets coming towards you in the dark, then passing overhead, was quite a feeling, I can tell you. Sitting or standing up was certainly not advisable!

We slept in a large three-storey house opposite the church with a straw palliasse to lay on, a straw pillow, and a blanket. It was a cold house, but the food was much better than what we could get at home.

When we had finished the course, that last evening we all went to the pub for a well-earned booze up. I felt on top of the world and the fittest that I had ever been. I knew that I was well trained for the job that would be needed, should the Germans land on English soil.

Back in Belstead, the Captain set our mobile patrol some night training exercises to see how good we were. The first task was to go to the anti-aircraft site between Wherstead and Belstead to pinch one of their shells. We had to crawl around the sentries to approach the shells which located close to the guns. One of us grabbed a round, crawled out, and the next day we took it to the blacksmiths shop, where George and Fred carefully dismantled it, and the captain took the primed shell case back to show the CO of the Ack-Ack unit.

Next, we had to infiltrate the searchlight base at Bentley to remove an article from their cookhouse. We were crawling in a ditch and froze solid when a sentry came along. It seems he'd been for a few drinks that evening (probably at The Case is Altered), and I got peed upon whilst we were silently laying there in the stinging nettles! I had to lie there and take it, and the sentry was none the wiser. We took some trophy back which our army captain returned to them, and he no doubt had a go at them for their lax security. Naturally, I never heard the end of the pee incident from the other chaps in my patrol!

The third exercise was to go to HMS *Ganges* to tie a sack on the outer railings of the mast. We didn't achieve that, as a big air raid started. We'd got as far as Chelmondiston, where they had 3.7 inch anti-aircraft guns to protect Shotley and Harwich. These big guns suddenly went off as we crawled close by, and it scared the living daylights out of us. When Mum did the laundry, she said "I knew you had coloured underpants, but not brown ones!"

After our special training, we passed on some of the knowledge to the normal home guard, holding back in the areas of sabotage and booby traps.

We all modified our shotgun ammunition, however. The idea was to take three twelve bore cartridges, remove the shot and wads, then we took half the charge from one to increase the powder in the two others. Then, we placed the top part of the wad onto the charge, and put a glass alley (large marble) in on top. With a .410 cartridge we would do much the same, but as an alley would not fit within, we used a steel ball bearing of the right size.

We reckoned that if a German was standing on the other side of the road and we fired a shotgun at him, what good would it be? It would hardly hurt him, let alone kill him. But a glass alley propelled by a charge-and-a-half would take him down at fifty yards.

My main weapon was a Browning automatic rifle, which held a clip of ten rounds that could be fired as a single shot or in a short burst. I was very proud to be given this weapon, perhaps as I was something of a crack shot? Also to hand was my old No. 1 shotgun which I'd converted into a bolt-action .22 by modifying the stock, shortening the barrel, and adding a bolt. (That gun is in the Parham museum.)

I had been taught all about the Mills bomb or hand grenade. There were different fuses: four or five seconds for house-to-house, where you pop it through the window; seven seconds for trench warfare; and eleven seconds for use with a grenade launcher. We could only throw a grenade 20 or 30 yards, but with the special attachments we were given for the end of the rifle, and a blank cartridge, we could project the bomb a hundred yards or more. I heard that some of the first silly buggers who tried one of these launchers put a real bullet in, rather than a blank, and that was the end of them! We had some of these launchers as part of our patrol equipment.

The Home Guard had a firing range down at Washbrook fens. I was teaching the chaps about fusing and throwing Mills bombs. You unscrew the bottom, put the fuse in and screw it back in. You then pull the safety pin so the lever pops out and the striker comes down. That hits the fuse and, depending on the time delay, you have a short while to get rid of it.

I was in a sandbag trench, and the other men were queuing up fifty yards behind me, coming in one at a time. They had already practised their throws with dummy bombs from our trench into the target trench, but now they were going to fuse and throw a live one.

Tubby Wilson, a lad of my age, dropped a live one! He leaned back to throw it in a cricket throw, but his arm hit the sandbags behind and jolted it out of his hand. We had already done the same throw with dummies, but I reckon that when he had a live one in his hand, he *really* wanted to be rid of it so he threw his arm back a bit further. Thankfully I was fast enough to grab it and fling it over the parapet before it went off. That could have been the end of us both. ♣

There was an Operational Base for the Secret Army. We had one in the Belstead Woods, and didn't know anything about how it got there, until we were introduced to it in 1941. It was built by army engineers and someone from the army took us down there one Sunday.

It was dug into a bank. The entrance was a crawl-in opening like a pill box, covered by holly trees. It was about ten feet wide and between fifteen and eighteen feet long. The escape tunnel went out the back with a wooden log screwed onto a three-foot wide steel plate; you turned the plate resting on the brick work, then it could be lifted.

We only went in it very occasionally so we did not leave tracks leading to it. It had six bunks, a table and bench, a corner end for weapons, explosives and supplies, and had a paraffin stove with a vent.

Harry Gladding was a friend of Dad's who lived next door and worked with him in Belstead Woods. In the early 1950s the pair of them were clearing tree stumps with dynamite, mainly oaks that had been cut at the beginning of the war for the war effort, as they wanted to replant the area. Dad had been in the Home Guard, but didn't know what I was doing other than being in a "mobile squad". They found the bunker well hidden in the woods. I don't know whether he already knew anything about its existence, but they blew it up with their dynamite, as they were worried the bulldozer might cave it in. It was a lot stronger than they expected, and bits of steel railway line, corrugated iron and vent pipes can still be seen.

If the invasion had happened, there were people in the village we would have to knock off. For me, not being religious, one of the top suspects was the parson! I thought he would be the number one collaborator to stop any fighting, because of his religion.

I was not there for the stand down of the unit, as I left for the RAF in 1943 and I never had much contact with the lads again. I don't even know who took my place when I left. I moved away to Bentley and then to Ipswich so I rarely saw the men again. I suppose they are all dead now and I must be the only surviving one around the area.

The son of George Junior, Dick Ward, was the last blacksmith in Belstead village as their business closed in the early 1960s.

Chapter 8
The ATC and desire to fly

As well as the Home Guard, I had joined the Air Training Corps in the newly formed 262 Squadron. (There was also at that time the 188 Squadron in Ipswich but we did not get on very well with them as we thought they were stuck-up townies! Many a fight took place between the different squadrons.) Most of our squadron came from the surrounding villages and the outskirts of town.

I now had thee uniforms: my ATC 262 squadron, the standard Home Guard uniform and for the Secret Army I had a dark green denim uniform, with no insignia or shiny stuff, along with rubber soled boots issue instead of the usual hobnails.

Early in 1940 both the ATC Squadrons went for a week's camp at nearby R.A.F. Wattisham. We learned how aircraft guns worked and about navigation and radio communications. Aircraft recognition was one of my favourite subjects, so I soon knew them all from any angle in those days. (That was how I instantly knew it was a Dornier 217 that dropped the Hermann.)

On that camp we were all taken up in a Bristol Blenheim aircraft for a ten-minute flight around the airfield. I was lucky enough to sit next to the pilot, and another young chap sat in the gunner's turret. When we came down we landed safely and were taxiing round for dispersal. In those days there were no hard runways at Wattisham, so we were on the grass when the tail wheel dropped into a deep rabbit hole. This broke the fuselage off behind the turret so we were cocked in the air, props up and still spinning! No harm done, as we were all able to walk away, but it was a bit alarming for my very first flight. ❧

That certainly did not put me off in the least. I had loved the flight and was desperate to join the RAF to get flying and help fight the Germans.

I was in a reserved occupation doing essential war work at Ransomes. I found I couldn't get away from there until I went and asked Mr Dick Stokes (MP for Ipswich) who was the co-owner, along with his brother who lived at Hintlesham Hall.

I booked appointments with his secretary to speak with him, and after about the third time of asking, he said he would release me.

Not many others were asking to go off from work that I knew of, only Bernard Jay who volunteered as air gunner. He got killed over Germany before I joined up. His brother also worked at Ransomes and told me the news when I was at work, but that didn't put me off. No other friends died in the war. The only other one I knew from Belstead was Danny Southgate. He was in the Royal Marines and died on HMS *Prince of Wales* when she was sunk in the Pacific. He was a bandsman; you still have fighting men to play music for services and parades, even on ships.

I went to the Barrack Corner recruiting office on May 3rd, 1943. As I cycled home to Belstead some stables were on fire in the village. Dad was helping the fire brigade so I stopped by to help too. When the fire was out, I said "Dad, I volunteered for the Air Force today." He smiled and said, "Did yer, boy? Good on yer!" And that was it. My mother did not seem bothered either way.

Granny wasn't very keen about me volunteering. Although she didn't say anything, I knew in her mind she did not like the idea of me leaving her on her own and probably not coming back.

As an RAF volunteer, I was the dream boy of the village I suppose, and all the girls were interested. I used to get lots of presents from them, and not all material, either!

Chapter 9
RAF Air Crew training

My medical was on 11th of May, then on the 18th I was away to Cardington for the attestation to see if I was suitable for Air Crew. This testing was held in the old Airship Hangars that are still there, and I believe they are now building a fancy new airship.

I came back home for a fortnight before going to the Aircrew Receiving Centre at St John's Wood in London where I was given all the injections and vaccinations. We all had to have two haircuts in two days, and could only assume the drill instructors were in league with the barber as we had to pay sixpence each time! Quite a racket, we thought. We collected our uniforms from a building at Lords Cricket Ground.

We were lads from all over the country but we all got on well together. The drill instructors gave us plenty of square bashing up and down the streets. I think the flats we were in were five or six stories high. The cookhouse was certainly in the basement, as I know this quite well!

I had been there a week or two when I was given a fortnight's "Jankers" for not reading the daily roster. On the Sunday, a perfectly good day off I thought, I went to see my Uncle Stan in Hounslow when I should have been on fire picket duty. When I returned I was confined to barracks, working in that cookhouse, peeling spuds and the like.

Then we were posted to Eastchurch in Kent for three weeks, and onwards to the Initial Training Unit (ITU) at Bridgnorth in Shropshire. At that time there were 39 pubs in the town. It was said you had not visited the place until you had done them all but that didn't pose us much of a problem!

We were taught King's Regulations with plenty of drill and Physical Training. One night I was asleep when some of the lads came in late and put a hedgehog in my bed. I rolled over onto it in the night and its spines pricked my penis and the lower part of my stomach. In the morning I was so badly swollen and enflamed that I had to go to sick quarters and stayed there three days. It was just a silly prank, and I just happened to be the victim, but as no one would own up to it, the whole hut was confined to barracks for a week. I was not very popular, but it was hardly my fault!

We were at Bridgnorth for about 12 weeks and in that time I made some good pals. I struggled to understand some of their accents, to start with. A most unusual accent was Mike Spery from North Cadbury in Somerset.

In those days I had a pretty ripe Suffolk accent myself, until I consciously started to drop it, so it was the same problem for everybody. I had never been out of Suffolk before the war, not even over into Essex. The only place I had seen a flush toilet before was in Waterloo Road, my maternal grandparent's place. (In Belstead we would simply empty our bucket in the garden to make the celery and rhubarb grow.)

Jimmy Simpson from Dundee was in the next bed of my billet. We both had strong accents but managed to understand each other and immediately hit it off. Jimmy had a clever trick where he could write Jimmy with his left hand while he wrote Simpson with his right. I have never known anyone else who could do that. He was my friend all along the way until we got posted into crews.

Another Scottish fellow, Jock Hamilton, said to us one day "There's a wee babeecoo!" All we English and Welsh had no idea what he meant until we saw he was looking at a calf!

45

I had been allocated the post of Wireless Op/Air Gunner by this time. The next posting was to No 4 Radio School at RAF Madley, near Hereford. This was very intense training on all aspects of radio communications, RADAR and Morse code over a 26-week period.

After about three weeks of classroom work we started air-to-ground communication. We flew up in a De Havilland Dominie, four of us at a time, with an instructor. We did about eight hours flying, learning how to communicate with ground stations and take direction findings using the DF loop. After passing this test we went on to fly in De Havilland Procters and Prentices, single-engine aircraft with a pilot and no instructor, doing the same thing until we became proficient on our own.

Of our initial intake Q25E, our unit of 25 men, we lost three in plane crashes in the Welsh hills. These training flights were piloted by single-seater fighter pilots on rest periods who took us up to practice, and I have no idea why they crashed like that.

We were fined half a crown if we lost our trailing aerial. There was a normal one fixed up on the aircraft, but for VHF it hung 30 feet out the back of the plane. This was a single wire with a brass ball on the end and half-inch lead balls along the length to keep it strung out behind. The wireless operator had to wind it out and in again on a drum, and if you forgot to wind it in before coming in to land, it would get caught up on telegraph poles or a hedge or something and you'd get fined for breaking it.

We did loads of Morse code practice, of course. Eight hours a day sending and receiving was not unusual. We had to get to 18 words a minute, then move on to 25 words. To pass our exam we had to manage 30 words a minute, as well as having all the electronic knowledge. I think there was automatic promotion for the other crew members after a year, from Sergeant to Flight Sergeant (with the crown), but this did not apply to the W/Op who first had to pass that Grade One Board exam.

We did a parachute collapsing drill, for when you land on the ground and your parachute is pulling you along and you need to collapse it quickly. I remember one day we did this in the summer time so we were only wearing singlets on top. One of the lads didn't manage to collapse his 'chute and it caught the wind and dragged him over the top of a Nissen hut, where the bolts are put up from the inside and the ends stick up through the roof. These studs tore his singlet off and scored his back very badly indeed. They stopped us doing parachute training in that location after this freak accident.

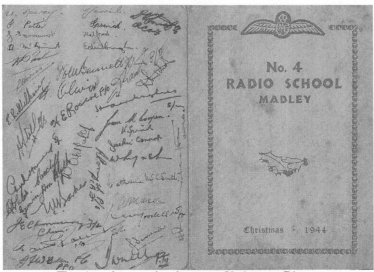

The signed menu for the 1944 Christmas Dinner

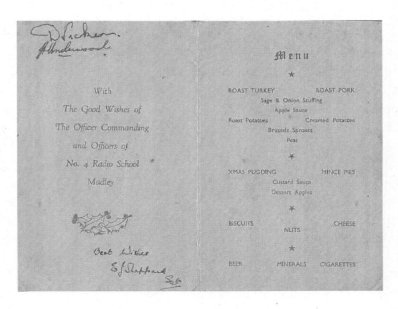

We had cubicles called Harwell Boxes where the equipment was laid out as it is in an aircraft. The instructor could create faults on your equipment and you would have to go in and find the particular problem. One time I went in and shut the doors behind me. I leaned forward to pick up the generator equipment at the bottom, but I hadn't switched it off! I got 750 volts and it threw me back off my chair through the double doors onto the floor outside. The instructor told me that would teach me to switch it off first! It was not so much the power of the shock, being only 750 milliamps, but the shock of it happening.

We all had to go on Sunday church parade, but they could not force you to go to the church. Those who didn't attend church had to wait outside, and an officer should wait with you, but they usually didn't want to do that. They wanted to go to church themselves, so they would dismiss us and let us go off. Jimmy and I were both of the same mind: head for the pub! We would walk the eight miles to Hereford and chat up the girls. As I always say, "The hungry must be fed".

Charging the 24 volt batteries and topping them up in the battery room was part of the training. It was a ground crew job to remove and charge them when you were on a squadron, but you had to understand all about the process. I clearly remember I was doing battery tests when it was announced over the tannoy that we had invaded Europe on 6th of June 1944.

At Mansell Lacy, six miles away from Madley, they brought in the first casualties from the beaches a week or so later. We were asked if we would visit the American wounded and write letters for them to send home to their families. We went there in the evenings to read to them and write their letters. I don't remember any of the men now, but certainly remember the terrible wounds they had. Some could not see, heads were all bandaged up, arms and legs were missing. Not very nice. Omaha beach was a trap for the Americans with all the fortifications still in place and the poor buggers were massacred. They did not talk about that.

We finished our radio course successfully.

RAF Madley, No 4 Radio School, Hereford. The day six of us passed out as W/Op and A/G. Top left – Osborne, Bob Prusher (Scotland), Self. Bottom: Jock Hamilton (Edinburgh), Jimmy Simpson (Dundee), Jennings.

I was back home on leave when, on September the 23rd 1944, I married my sweetheart Sally Gordon whom I had been courting for over two years. It was a great wedding as her sister married an American airman at the same time, making it a unique occasion, the joining up of personnel from two great air forces on the same day.

During the reception in Ipswich we had seven flying bomb warnings but none of them crashed in our area. These were very scary times as you did not know when or where they might suddenly come down. We spent our wedding night at my parent's house in Belstead and spent happy times together for the rest of my week's leave.

Back on duty, we were put in a holding pool for eleven weeks, staying on at Madeley. They had got no new posting for us, as the Gunnery schools were full up or something. We did all sorts of cross-country, both in planes, and on foot! We had cross-country running competitions to keep us fit and I was the champion.

The SAS from Malvern took us out in a lorry in the woods in the Black Hills for three days survival training. We were together as a crew with just an old parachute harness between us, and an instructor showed us how to survive on our own. That's where I had dandelion and earthworm soup. There's nothing wrong with worms, and it's surprisingly good meat, as long as you wash all the earth out of them with water before cooking.

Then followed a posting up to 10 (Observer) Advanced Flying Unit at RAF Dumfries in 1945 for an air gunnery course, this time flying in Avro Ansons equipped with a pair of .303 guns in a single turret. That was great fun! I really enjoyed flying over the Irish Sea, firing at a drogue towed by another aircraft. We took three or four passes on it, then they brought it down and counted the holes and patched them up for the next test. I got one of the highest marks they had had in a while, with eleven hits on a drogue. The usual tally was three or fewer. Just damned luck of course!

During that course we joined a square search off the Isle of Man looking for the crew of a B-17 Flying Fortress which had come down in the sea. One of the other crews found them in their dinghy. We also saw Barracuda aircraft depth-charging for what we assumed was an enemy submarine.

Flying time at gunnery school was about thirty hours and I passed my course with no problem.

Chapter 10
My crews and a spell in the "Glasshouse"

N ext stop was at RAF Wing, near Leighton Buzzard, to "crew up". We assembled in the Sergeant's Mess where I was approached by a pilot, Flight Sergeant John Haigh, who asked me to become his WOP/AG as he assembled his crew. We did about twenty trips together doing cross-country flights, high level bombing and fighter evasive action. We also flew from Edgehill, Morton-in-the-Marsh, Banbury and Chipping Norton to give us experience of different airfields. Why we moved around so much for the different parts of the training, I don't know. At Edgehill I remember weather observations where they sent a balloon up for us to watch with binoculars to observe how it behaved in the wind at different heights.

We were then posted to No 26 Operational Training Unit (OTU), back at RAF Wing again, for further training. This was in May 1945 when the war in Europe ended. We were given a week's leave to celebrate and then carried on with our training.

The Navigation Section at RAF Wing, by the way, had a motto on the wall "MAN IS NOT LOST". Some wag had written underneath it "but occasionally is completely unaware of his exact location".

A little while later we were pleased to get issued a weekend pass. However, on the Friday, the corporal in charge of the RADAR section said that he considered we were a little unsure of the theory of a new system called LORAN, so he wanted us back on Saturday morning for some extra tuition. We thought, "Sod that for a lark!" The six of us were not very keen and talked about not attending, but the others all stayed and it was only me who went off home on the Friday night. I had only been married a few months, and "There's that thing in life that will draw you further than gunpowder will blow you" so I wanted the weekend off that I had been promised! When I reported back on the Sunday night I was put under close arrest for being absent without leave. I was in a cell for the night and had to report to the CO next morning.

He said "Sergeant, this will not do at all. I am taking you out of your crew and you will go to RAF Norton to brush up on your RAF discipline." Everybody knew what RAF Norton was, it was the aircrew "glasshouse" near Sheffield where everyone who misbehaved was sent.

On arriving at the camp guardroom, our new intake was met by a Redcap Squadron Leader who said "Welcome, Gentlemen, and by the way, that's the last time that you will be called that while you are here. The Air Force has not demoted you, but in here you will be known as airmen and will be under the care of my corporal, and you will address him as 'Sir' regardless of your rank." This was a shock, as we were all a higher rank than him, from Sergeants up to Flight Lieutenants. I mean, some of the chaps had done a tour or more of Ops, and were here just for untidy uniforms or a brawl in the Mess!

He carried on, "This is a three-week intensive course of RAF discipline. Everywhere at the double, from 6 o'clock in the morning until 10 o'clock at night. There will be roll call every hour and do not be late or you will find that I am not the forgiving kind."

We did square bashing, rifle drill, plenty of PT and a lot of administration lessons on the King's Regulations and mock court martials.

We also did nightguard duty, with six of us on the front gate and six at the back. The back post was much preferred as it was next to the WAAF quarters, where some of us managed to spend a bit of time during guard duty! It was lights out at ten each night but we still played cards by torch light and made or lost a few quid.

On our third week we were allowed to go into Sheffield in the evenings, from 6 o'clock until midnight. We went to The Crown pub near the railway station. The bloke who owned the pub was the brother of a corporal up at Norton. He reserved a corner specially for us which was known as the Clueless Clots Club. To be a full member you had to bite the tip off your tie, dip it in your beer, flick it up and make it stick on the ceiling.

On those evenings we made up for lost time. We boozed and had great fun with the local girls, who knew very well we had plenty of money, as we had been inside for two weeks! Some of the girls really knew their way around and many a liaison was carried out in the bombed-out buildings near the railway station. I was married, but so what! Life was life! In those days we were out to have as much fun as possible while we still could.

At a quarter to twelve each night the taxi boys would be outside waiting to take us back to camp quickly, as we were not allowed to be a minute late or that meant another week inside with no privileges.

I didn't make any particular friends at RAF Norton, but a chap asked me, "Do you know who that is in the bunk next to you?" I had no idea, as I was not into football, but he was apparently a well-known Arsenal player, but I can't remember his name.

On the Friday of the third week, the good boys were posted back to their unit, taking back a sealed report of the stay at "the glasshouse". We were not given any particular time to report back to our unit. I was issued a rail pass which stated: "From Sheffield to ..." and there, it was blank. So, I went home via Peterborough to Ipswich and stayed the weekend with Sally.

I went back to RAF Wing on the Sunday night and handed in my report. On Monday morning I had to see the Station W/O, who said "You have done quite well, you have got 86% on all these subjects. I hope you have learned from your mistake. There is no crew available for you just now, so you will have to wait until someone needs a wireless op."

Things had not stood still, of course, when I had been away. Haigh had been allocated a new W/Op to replace me and they all moved to RAF Swinderby. Haigh had a mate called Flying Officer Prince, who found himself without his W/Op when the chap went home on compassionate leave after his family were killed in a bomb raid.

Prince needed to do a last cross-country trip to complete the training, so he asked Haigh if he could borrow his new W/Op. They went on the trip and, on their return, were told to change runway direction because of a wind change. They went off towards the Wash to circle round and they were never heard of again. It was assumed they went down in the Wash, possibly shot down by one of the Junkers 88 that used to come to raid the training areas and catch the bombers coming in to land.

That was another lucky escape for me. I should have been on board with them, had I not been sent to the Glasshouse. ✤

Whilst waiting for my own new crew I was put in charge of No. 6 camp site, which was just a bunch of Nissen huts billeting airmen. This was a very easy duty, as all I had to do was to inspect it to see that the other airmen kept their billets and the site clean and tidy. I was soon terribly bored, as I'd had nothing to do for a couple of weeks and we'd had no inspections ourselves. There was an old boy there in his fifties who reminded me of my Dad. I think he was just called up for something to do, and he did nearly all the work keeping the place ship-shape.

I said to him, "We haven't seen anyone yet. How often do you think they will inspect this place?" He said, "They never come here." I said "Really? Then I'm going home this weekend. Here's a ten-bob note. I have written down some instructions. If I am needed for anything, send a telegram to that address with the words 'Your horse is running tomorrow' so I will know I need to be back on the very first train."

I was home for nearly a fortnight! I was friendly with one of the WAAF Flight Sergeants at Head Quarters, who had lost her husband to the war. Being friendly with those ladies was good, as it meant I could often get passes out and ration cards. As can be seen from the photos of me in those days, the charm was there!

When the telegram arrived, I sped back to RAF Wing. The old chap said he heard on the tannoy that I was to report to HQ as soon as possible. This I did and was told that a new crew had arrived and required a W/Op.

The pilot, Sqn Ldr Geoffrey Knowles, had done a tour on Bostons, a tour on Mosquitos and had been a backup photographic pilot for the Armiens Prison Raid (Operation Jericho). With us on the Wellingtons was F/Lt Paddy Drenhan as bomb aimer, Jack Page as flight engineer, F/Sgt Johnny Marsden was the navigator, F/O Keith Skeets was rear gunner, and P/O Jack Cunliffe was mid-upper gunner. Jack was 38, and a real old boy who used to play for St Helens. He would say to us, "You haven't played rugby until you can do this!" He'd put his hand up and take all his teeth out. "That was what they did in the scrum," he said, "First time in, fist in the face and that was it, bye-bye teeth."

We did all our training on Wellingtons at 26 OTU. I have to say Knowles was not a lot of fun and was right into his discipline. If an airman passed and did not salute him he blew his top. Johnny Marsden would be told "Get that Airman and bring him to me" and he'd get a proper dressing down. He was from the University Air Squadron at Oxford and spoke very posh, putting "What?" with almost everything. The funny thing was he had done two tours of Ops and all he had was the Air Efficiency Medal and bar. That was a green ribbon with white strip, with a star on his. It seemed unusual to have no DFC or similar after all those Ops.

There were a few incidents along the way, naturally. We did dinghy drills in the old flooded sand pits nearby. One of the chaps started screaming like mad. We hauled him out of the water to find the calf of his leg was raked and bleeding, as he had been bitten by a huge pike. Their sharp teeth turn backwards and it had had ripped lots of skin off his leg. We didn't do that drill in there anymore!

The main incident was during fighter affiliation training, to learn evasion in flight and for the gunners to try to shoot down the enemy. We had a Hurricane that came at us, the gunners had camera guns on and when the fighter came into attack the gun trigger is pressed and it takes a movie of the attacker. Our pilot would do the corkscrew, left and right. When we landed the films were developed and available for viewing the results within half an hour, so we could see what the gunners would have hit.

We were doing this fighter affiliation training one day and, as Knowles was new to Wellingtons, he was flying dual. The Instructor Pilot, W/O Powell, asked Knowles if he had ever done an unassisted approach. This is where you are running out of fuel so you have to land and can't go round again. You cut the throttles right back to save fuel, stall down until you nearly hit the runway and then push the throttles right through the gate to full power, hoping there is enough fuel left to level you out. The instructor misjudged this horribly and touched us down so hard that we bounced back up into the air and damaged the undercarriage. He kept us flying and circled around. We tried in vain to get the undercarriage to go down. The hydraulic pressure didn't do it, so we tried the emergency air-bottle backup, but that was no good either. The Hurricane flew below us to check the damage and he told us over the R/T that the wheels were bent back.

The pilots agreed they would have to make a belly landing on the grass at the side of the runway, so I jettisoned the fuel. It was one of the wireless operator's jobs to call out how much fuel we had left and to press the jettison button. Knowles got us to take up the crash positions and Powell landed on the grass to avoid sparks. When we touched down, the undercarriage totally collapsed and we skidded along on our belly until we came to a halt near the control tower. The aircraft was a complete write-off. I split my head open at the top, but mine was the only injury. Everyone got out safely, and the wireless op is always the last out. Any air crash you can get out and walk away from is a lucky one! ♣

It was not Knowles' fault, it was the instructor's fault, as he was flying it and it was his daft idea! At the inquiry it was agreed that the pilot had misjudged the first attempt at landing, not realising that we had still got a lot of fuel on board and he was just given a reprimand.

The entry in my log book

58

We then went home on three weeks leave and were told to report to RAF Swinderby in Lincolnshire, to join No 6 Heavy Conversion Unit where we started flying Avro Lancaster four-engine bombers.

I well remember the big information poster up in the Mess. It had a picture of a Lancaster going off the end of a runway with the warning words "Conserve your brake pressure". Someone had added below it "... is all very good, but at the end of 05 is a bloody great wood!"

Knowles didn't obviously pay enough attention to the advice on that poster, as we did go off Runway 05 one day. I am not a pilot but assume we didn't have enough brake pressure. We went right off over the perimeter track and nearly into the public road, but not as far as the wood, thankfully. It was a bumpy excursion but no real damage was done, and our Lanc just had to be towed back. ♣

We finished our Lancaster conversion course, thinking we may be sent out to the war still going in the East, but that didn't happen.

Knowles stuck his hand up for us to do ferry trips. We would nip over in an Avro Anson to Aldergrove in Belfast, pick up a new Lanc built in Canada, all pure white at that time ready for painting, and we would ferry them back to various places.

We did a few of these trips. On the very last Lancaster flight we did, in March 1946, we came in to land at Manchester, where the skipper turned around too sharpish and the left wheel strayed off the concrete and sank into the soft soil. That tipped us enough that we couldn't go any further, which was a bit of a limp ending to my flying career.

We were made redundant from flying after I had done over two hundred hours training and no Ops and was never actually posted to a squadron, which meant of course I got no decoration other than the usual war service medals. At the time I was disappointed that I had not achieved what I had trained so hard to do, but looking back, I was of course terribly lucky. ♣

Chapter 11
Post War and Demob

I remained in the RAF for another 13 months after we finished flying. I stayed on at Swinderby and was put in charge of the parachute cloakroom, where we issued the flying gear and parachutes for the training crews who had taken over.

The crews would take a parachute and then bring it back after each trip, and we also managed lots of spare replacement gear like helmets, flying suits, boots and harnesses. Every so often the WAAFs took the parachutes to the parachute repacking section that each airfield had, where they would be checked and repacked on a fifty-foot bench.

With six of us in the cloakroom doing that job, we found we were very overstaffed. It was a lovely cushy job, the easiest one I ever had. The officer in charge was P/O Phillips, who came in and said "Here we are boys, I know you buggers are all like me and eager to get out. I have got these shoes down here and I am the only ones walking on them. So don't tread on my toes!" He went on, "I know what you are going to do, so I will tell you anyway. There will be three of you on duty one week, three of you at home, and then *vice versa*."

We had rations to collect every night, being a quarter of tea, a pound of sugar, a loaf of bread, and string of sausages or the like to collect from the cook house for our own little cooking area. I went to the cook house one day, where a young airmen called Joe Cawston was in charge. He was a Suffolk boy as well, and said "I'm in a bit of a muddle, look here, I have half a side of beef left over. Do you want a bit? I have to get rid of it."

He cut some great big lumps off it, and me and the others each took as much home in a suitcase as we could. I shared that meat around all the family when I got home and was most popular. Funnily enough, when I went to work on the railway I was in the Ipswich yard when I saw this chap who said, "I know you!" Joe had got a job as shunter, too.

I had some good fortune another time at Swinderby. I was friendly with a chap in HQ who was also redundant air crew. He came by with a little box, about six inches square and three inches deep. "There you are," he said to us, "I want a tenner for this." Now that was a lot of money then, but we found it was a box of 72-hour ration cards. There must have been a gross of them in there to share between six of us. He said "I've stamped two or three of them, nice and deeply. You know what to do. Get a potato, cut it in half and wipe it dry, then press it on one of my stamps and stamp that onto the next card."

People were helping themselves in those days a bit, now the war was over. If I knew then what I know now, I could be a millionaire.

For instance, they were chucking the 1154 and 1155 radio transmitters and receivers into pits and running them in with bulldozers. Those receiver and transmitters were worth a lot of money, perhaps thirty or forty quid, when your wages were only three quid a week. There were piles of surplus stuff buried, such as torches and batteries. What a terrible waste. I was told that the Yanks at RAF Raydon chucked 500 bicycles in a pit and buried them before they left! It is hard to understand the logic of that.

A chap came to join us in the parachute cloakroom, and he slung a big sack in the corner with an 8-inch jaw engineer's vice in it. He said, "I will try to get that home one of these times." I suggested the first one to get it home should have it and I had it home in a flash. My brother still uses it in his workshop now.

There was a bit of a swindle on the railway that a chap told us about, as there was a clever forger on the base. You would go to Lincoln and buy a three-month open ticket to Sleaford. You also bought a ticket from Lincoln to Colchester. Every time you travelled on the railway, the ticket collector would come along to punch out the shape – a square, a diamond, a star and other shapes – and we would pick these pieces up off the floor once he had gone. I got out at Ipswich and said I was breaking my journey up, so I never actually went as far as Colchester nor gave my ticket up. When we went back to Newark, there was usually such a rush of people going off that they never had a chance to collect all the tickets in, so I would hang on to my ticket.

I would take the tickets and the punch outs to this man who was damned clever. He would take the tickets and slice them in half, stick the open return on the back of the Colchester ticket and force the little patterns back in. For that job he charged half a crown each time, so I could go home for a weekend for very little money. We did not have a military travel pass, of course, when we were skiving off!

The winter of 1946-47 was one of the worst for many years and the snow remained for over three months. We were running out of coke at Swinderby as our station commander had sent half our supply to our local satellite station a few miles away, as they had already run out.

I was put in charge of about a dozen airmen to cut down a copse of trees on the edge of the airfield and cut them into logs for the central heating boilers. Each morning we went out in a lorry armed with saws and axes, and a full ration of bacon, eggs and bread for the day. The first thing we did was to set up a cooking area and, being a country boy, it suited me very well. We cut up dozens of logs which were transported back to camp by lorry. We did this for about a month until we got a new supply of coke in.

On one of my days off I decided to hitch a lift down into Lincoln on the Fosse way, which is a straight road with a six-foot ditch either side, which was deep with snow at this time. Lucky or not, I was picked up by two men in a large American Studebaker car. As they sped on into town they misjudged the overtaking of a small Post Office van, and clipped a lorry coming the other way. We landed upside down in the ditch where we could not get out, all very shaken but none of us was hurt. ♣

An elderly couple in a little Austin Seven car chugged along and stopped to help. Our rescuers had to smash the rear window to release us. I can see her face today, this dear little old lady as she asked me if I still wanted to carry on to Lincoln. I did, and they took me into a café there and bought me a cup of tea. I suspected that she had been a nurse and wanted to see if I was alright After a chat we finished our tea and went our separate ways and I will always fondly remember that generous couple.

The snow eventually cleared and the flying started again, so I was back to my job in the parachute cloakroom once again. One night I broke into the map room to "borrow" some maps for a friend. Whilst in there I heard the key in the door so I hid between the lockers. In came the duty officer with the WAAF duty officer who proceeded to make passionate love on the office desk! This was where my stealth training came in, as I was able to keep perfectly still and quiet during their love-making. If I had been caught it would have certainly meant a court martial for me.

Only one time was I really drunk in the RAF. I was coming back to Swinderby from Lincoln after a night out with friends. I'd had too much to drink, so when I jumped off the bus I went straight into the ditch at the side of the Fosse way, and got my best blues covered in mud! I was in charge of church parade the next day so I had to wash it all and dry it out in the boiler room that night, ready for the morning, and didn't get a lot of sleep.

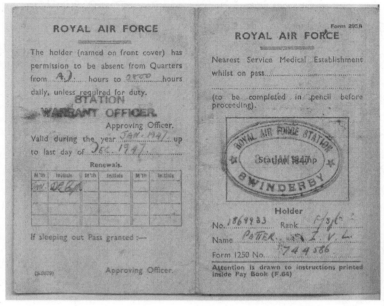

Weekend Pass Book

At Lincoln there was a nurse training school and we would meet the nurses in the summer, then hire a skiff on the river for a couple of hours for half a crown. I went with a chum and we met up with two girls. I rowed up while he cuddled her, then we got to Stamford, and I said, "Your turn!" It was then that the bugger told me he couldn't row! I had to row home as well and never got a cuddle with my girl. That was six miles on the river and I wouldn't ever make that mistake again. I had only learned to row myself whilst there, but it came totally naturally to me. We had never been in boats at the River Stour, only paddling.

I certainly liked to chase the girls, as did many of us. Each station had an ETR – early treatment room – which were little block houses away from the main camp. If you had been out with the girls, you went there first for a check of the meat and two veg. They had a wash basin and cream to put down inside your old fella. You did that just in case. Those that didn't, they might get a rash a bit later on and would have to go to sick quarters. We used condoms but you still caught other things as well. It all depended on how fast you were and if it was for half a crown or free! (I didn't pay often, that was a last resort.)

I was demobbed from Swinderby on 7 May 1947. I was given a suit in a box but came out with my uniform. I kept the tunic and eventually wore out my two pairs of RAF trousers working on the railway. I don't remember what happened to my best blue jacket, but when I heard a few years ago that they had no NCO's battledress blouse at Flixton Air Museum, I sent them mine.

All fit air crew were put on reserves for 6 months, and then some were given the option to sign on for longer, but I didn't wish to do that. I had a job and was settled down by then, so that was the end of my RAF career.

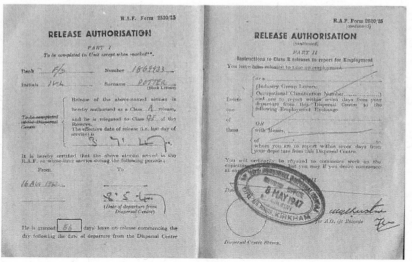

Chapter 12
Sally and Sonia

S ally Gordon was my sweetheart whom I married. We first met when I was working for the Plumbs, delivering telegrams. They were quite regularly sent to the local mansion, Belstead House, where Sally was a parlour maid. She would come to the door with her little silver tray and I would wait to see if there was a reply. I loved chatting up the girls and was well known for that! I had flirted with her a bit at the doorway and was quite sweet on her, and I had decided I might ask her out some time.

In 1942 I went to the Regent Cinema to watch a film, but don't ask me what it was. I can't remember anything about it, as events overtook it! This young girl came along on her own and the usherette happened to sit her in beside me. I didn't know who it was until the lights went up at the interval, when I recognised Sally and said that I knew her from Belstead House. We got talking and I offered to walk

her home. She had left service by then and was doing war work on a lathe at Ransomes. That chance meeting was a real stroke of luck! ☘

We arranged for me to pay a visit to 50 Rosehill Road one evening to meet her parents, and at that time we arranged a date. On that first date we went for a walk in Holywells park, and I still have the half bus ticket from that happy day.

Sally and her sister Betty were orphans who came over together from Ireland when they were about six. They went to Dr Barnardos at Brentwood, where they were treated very badly.

65

(Actually, they were not quite orphans, but two of a number of sisters from different fathers, I understand.)

When they were aged about nine they were adopted by William and Gertrude Fitch, who then brought them up in Ipswich. Mr and Mrs Fitch were wonderfully kind and delightful people. They had a biological son called Lionel, who became my best man.

Mr Fitch was a "Saw Doctor". He cut up all the big bits of rough timber on the saws and maintained all the saw machinery. At the time I met him he was working at Tibenhams, a woodworkers and furniture makers near St Peters Church and Stoke Bridge. Sally was asked to go in and help paint the little white crosses that were sent over to mark graves for men killed in action overseas. She was a young, newly married girl with a husband in Bomber Command, so I wasn't best pleased about her doing that job, but she didn't seem to mind. Tibenhams closed after the war and Mr Fitch moved to Ransomes, where this picture of him was taken.

(This is not my photo but it has no marking and I have no way to credit it.)

Mrs Fitch had kept the sweet shop in High St, near where the museum is, before they moved to Rosehill Rd. They then moved to 521 Bramford Lane, Ipswich which was later bequeathed to Sally and we moved in there ourselves in 1958.

Mr and Mrs Fitch

I am not a tall man, about 5 foot 8, but Sally was 5 foot nothing and tucked in under my chin. One day, we had visited the Fitches and when we were leaving, Sally was standing on tiptoes in the lounge, looking in the mirror to check her hair. I said, "You can't really see, can you?" and I put my hands around her waist and lifted her up. She was light as a feather and I lifted her a bit too high, so that her head knocked and broke the big light, which was a lovely pink and white glass globe hanging on three chains above! Sally was not hurt, thankfully, but I feel that Mrs Fitch never quite forgave me for that.

As I mentioned, our wedding was on 23rd September 1944 at Trinity Church, Ipswich, at the bottom of Bishop's Hill. Sally married me and I had Lionel Fitch, my future brother-in-law, as my best man. At the same time, Sally's sister Betty married Nick Sampson, a US airman. His best man I only remember by his nickname "Shoes", as I only met him the once and never saw him again. I believe this was a unique occasion, being the only time that the two air forces were joined at a double wedding.

Betty and Nick Sampson went off to the States after the war, and we went to stay with them at South Weymouth in Boston for a fortnight during our six-week visit to USA. They came over to visit us once, as well. There was a B17 that crashed at Framlingham. Nick took the instruments out and gave the clock to our father-in-law, Mr

Fitch. It was a lovely piece of mahogany, the same that was used in panelling the *Queen Mary*, I was told.

Our first home together was 92 Whitton Church Lane, which was a new council house acquired by Mr Fitch for his son. Lionel was in RAF ground crew, somewhere in the desert in Africa, where he was machine-gunned and injured in the legs. Whilst he was convalescing in Loughborough, we made us of the house.

Sally was there about three or four months, mainly on her own as I was still away in the RAF. One day I remember we went down to one of the river mouths with the Fitches and brought back a pail of winkles. You have to put them in salt water overnight so they clean themselves, so we put them under the sink but we didn't think to put anything on top of the pail. When we came down in the morning we found they had all got out and we were crushing them underfoot everywhere, so as it turns out nobody ate any of them!

Lionel and his wife came to live there and their first son Bobby was born. (They went on to have a daughter Janet and two more sons, Richard and Peter.) Sally moved in with Mrs Fitch's sister in Shakespeare Road. She lived there for five months, and that's where Sally went into labour with our daughter, Sonia, in 1946.

Sally moved to Bentley Old Hall with Granny Kate during the bad winter of 1946-47 where there were huge snow drifts all around. She had to melt snow to get water, and heat it up to wash nappies and things. She decided she hated the countryside after all that!

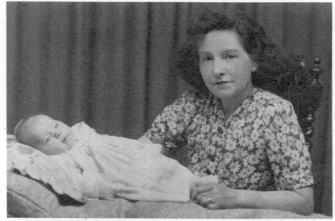

Sonia with Mrs Fitch

Mr Fitch had a moped, and he took Sally on the back for a ride one day. They went down from Washbrook and up Swan Hill to Sproughton. She was so light that when she fell off the back he didn't even notice! She was not hurt, fortunately. ❧

Sally's real name was Sarah but she didn't like being called that one bit. It was the quickest way to bring up her Irish temper! We were married for 53 years and had a very happy marriage. We had our daughter, Sonia, but then Sally didn't want any more children.

At that time, after the war work in factories was over, Sally went to work at British Sugar's sugar beet factory at Sproughton. When the lorry loads came in she had to pick out about a dozen samples from each lorry to test them for sugar content in the laboratory. I was not going to let her keep doing that job, clambering on the lorries, after she was pregnant. When Sonia was born she went back to work at Holly Farm at Copdock, pruning and picking fruit, for about four years.

I got to know the farmer there, Mr Dunt, and his daughter's pet donkey! By 1954 I was going into work by motorcycle, to save a lot of time and pedalling. One evening, going past Holly Farm on my way to my night shift, this donkey ran out of a side road in Copdock, knocking me off and causing a lot of damage to my 250cc BSA, but I was unhurt. ♣

The farmer was trying to catch the beast at the time, so he saw what happened and helped me up. He apologised, saying, "That bloody donkey will be the death of me, or someone else! Wherever I put him the sod will always get out."

Mr Dunt helped me wheel my bike to the side of the road and, after catching the donkey, he took me to work in his car. He said he would be there at six o'clock the next morning to take me home. This he did, and took me to work and back for the next night shift too, by which time my brother Michael had got my bike repaired and Mr Dunt paid for all the work. Despite that incident, I have always loved donkeys and give money to the donkey sanctuary.

We still used to love to go to Stutton shore. In those days I would take my family down by road on my motorbike, needing three trips each way. First grandma on pillion with my dog Judy on the tank, then I would pick up Sonia, then one last trip to pick up Sally. We went on the road about 3½ miles all the way to Stutton Village hall, after which it became just a cart track when we headed past Fison's Manor to Stutton point. Other villagers and their children came down to the shore. Sometimes there would be twenty or more people down there on Sundays and the four Bank Holidays, if the weather was good.

Our daughter Sonia never learned to drive a car, only motorbikes. She had a Francis Barnett like I'd had, and a little BSA Bantam. Sonia married Michael in 1973 and they have three children: Lee, Kevin and Michelle, and I have a great-grand-daughter as well!

Poor Sally fell ill with a massive abdominal growth in 1997. When they operated they realised it was not curable, so they never even sewed her up again, just bandaged her as best they could. She could not communicate as she was unconscious under morphine and she passed away the next night.

Sonia's wedding day

I went to Sally's funeral alone, as that was how we wanted it. We wanted a plain casket and I insisted there must be no brass on the coffin. I said she had cleaned enough of that when she was in service, and we don't want any more! The undertaker said I had to have a name plate on it, by law.

I had her cremation as late as possible in the day. I told them "Bring the coffin in, I will follow it, and you will place it on the dais. I will say goodbye and when you draw the curtains I will take my leave." But when the chap shut the curtains I was rigid. I could not move, until he took hold of my arm and led me away, and then I drove myself home.

We had agreed we should never be on our own if anything happened to the other. I have certainly always made sure I found someone to talk to.

Sally on Stutton Shore

A happy family at the seaside

Chapter 13
On the Railways, ganging & shunting

My demob was on 20th of May 1947, after which I had planned to follow a family tradition in the police force. I had already been allowed leave from the RAF to go down to Peel House in London to pass the preliminary police exams. Once I got back home, I went to St Helens Gaol in Ipswich to apply to join the Suffolk Police. I showed my documents to the Sergeant.

He looked at the papers, then looked at me and said, "Sorry, son. You won't get in the Suffolk Police now, as they have just put the height up from 5'8 to 5'9. But you can get in the Metropolitan Police at your height, if you like." "No thanks!" I said, feeling very dejected.

As I was biking home, I encountered an old friend of the family, Bill Butcher, who was cycling home from his work on the Belstead Railway Gang. He said "So you're out then, boy? What are you doing now?" I explained my disappointment with the police and that I did not want to go back to working inside a factory again.

"Well," he said, "You have worked as an engineer so why not try and work on the railways? There are jobs going as plate layers and that's a good outdoors job. Go and see Bob Whatling, the chief engineer at Ipswich Station, and tell him I sent you."

That is what I did the very next day. Mr Whatling said, "You are just out of the forces, so you must be fit enough. On Friday the medical coach will be here in Ipswich. I assume you will pass that alright as you haven't been injured, have you?"

The medical coach went round the area with a doctor on board to check out all the staff and potential recruits. I went down on the Friday and when I sailed through that I went straight in to tell Mr Whatling. He said, "Good! You can start work on Bentley Station, as a plate layer. Call and see Mr Parker the station master on Monday morning at 7:30, and he will introduce you to the plate-laying gang."

This I did on the 6th of June 1947, which I call my D-day. It was the start of a long and enjoyable career of 39 years. I felt very lucky that I had bumped into that old boy who suggested the job on the railways. ♣

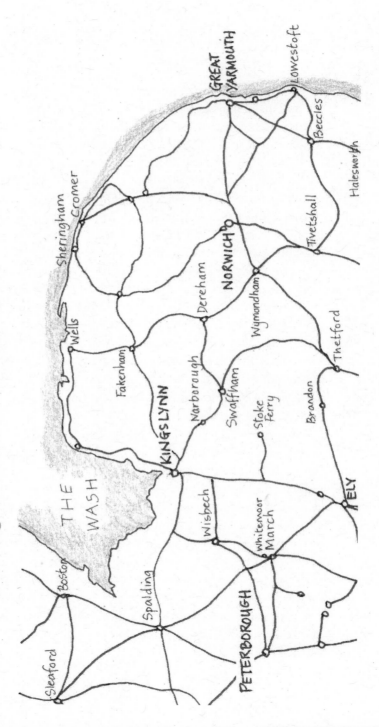

East Anglian Rail Network circa 1950

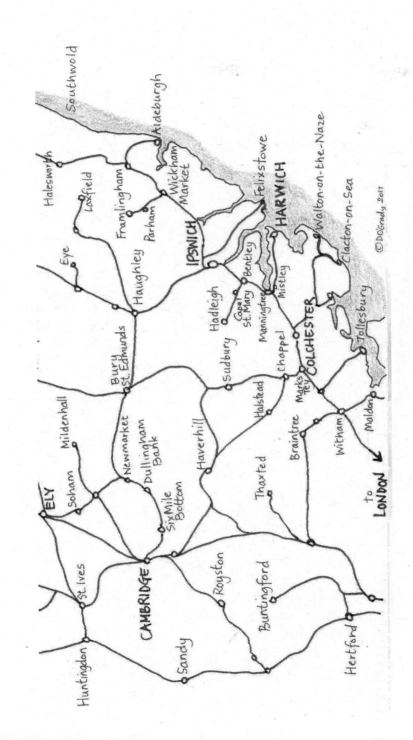

I enjoyed every moment of my career, apart from the first few days, perhaps. My hands were so soft after being in the Air Force, with little hard manual work to do, that I came home at night so blistered I could hardly open up my hands.

Mr Parker took me to meet the ganger called Harry Holmes who was 63 and had served in the 1914-18 war. The gang consisted of sub-ganger Harry Barrell, who had not been in the services, and two platelayers Stan Butcher and Harry Sergant, who had both been in the army and demobbed about six months earlier. I joined them as a third platelayer at Bentley and got paid £4-4s a week.

As a small gang we had to look after three miles of the main track which ran between Ipswich and London and part of the branch line which ran from Bentley Junction to Hadleigh. We had five huts on our section made from old railway sleepers. We used these to store the tools and sit in for meals on cooler days. Each hut had an open fire which became very welcome during the cold weather.

I was given a shovel and pick, then off we went to start packing the ballast under some track that had been re-laid the day before, to make it firm and level. I remember the first three sleepers I put the ballast under, right at the edge of the station, as if it were only yesterday.

This was very hard work for me as I had not done much decent manual work for four years. We stopped for about a half an hour for lunch break, which usually consisted of bread and cheese and cold tea from an old beer bottle.

We also used a tool called a beater, which was like a pick with a blunt end. As the new track was about a mile long, we were joined by 60 other men and it still took us a week to make it safe for trains to travel at the track speed of seventy miles an hour.

The track laying was more skilful than people might think. All the wheels were fixed to the axles, which means on a curve the outer wheel would have to move further than the inner, so it would slip and cause wear to both the rail and the wheel. To get round this problem, all the wheel rolling surfaces were angled so that the inner part of the wheel, by the flange keeping it inside the tracks, was a greater diameter than the outer part. The rails were laid with a cant on all

76

the curves, which would cause the wheels to angle themselves in that way, and also steer the train automatically round the bends.

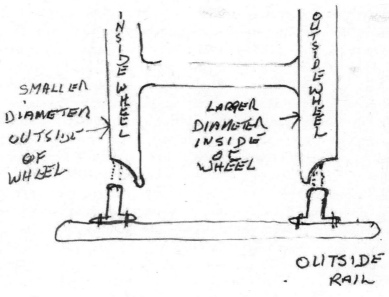

SMALLER
DIAMETER
OUTSIDE
OF
WHEEL

LARGER
DIAMETER
INSIDE
OF
WHEEL

INSIDE WHEEL

OUTSIDE WHEEL

OUTSIDE
RAIL

Stan's picture demonstrating how the wheels negotiated corners

After about a month I was allowed to work on Sundays, when they judged I had sufficient knowledge of railway work. I had to cycle to the engineering depot at Ipswich by about 6 am to catch the train and ride out to where the job was, anywhere within a 30-mile radius of Ipswich. We worked until about 5 pm, it was then back to the depot by train and cycling home again to Bentley. A long day of hard work, but this was worth another twelve to fifteen shillings a week in pay. There was always plenty of Sunday work and this greatly helped with the cost of living.

One of the Sunday jobs was to repair and wash out the drain culvert that ran between the tracks in Ipswich tunnel. This had not been done since it was built in the previous century. The culvert was about four feet square and was silted up by the ash that dropped from fireboxes of steam engines.

I worked with another platelayer. It was a filthy job and we wore special rubber suits. A hole had to be broken through about every thirty feet to gain access. We each got into a hole and pushed a long steel rod though, with a wire on it attached to a bucket. We pulled this backwards and forwards until we had cleaned out the silt between the two holes. It took twenty-five consecutive Sundays working eight hours a day to complete this job through the length whole tunnel. We were paid for an extra two hours over what we actually did each Sunday, a bonus that we certainly earned.

Each day a ganger had to walk the three miles of track in both directions to ensure that there were no obstructions or broken rails and that the wooden keys that held the rails in place were secure.

In 1949 I was offered a Railway Cottage near Bentley station, for a rent of £3-3-6, on the basis of me being a callout man. I had to be available should a train driver report that he had hit something on the track, which would have to be inspected before the next train was allowed to pass. There were loose horses, sheep, cows and deer that strayed onto the tracks at times. Even if the driver only hit an animal as small as a fox, he would know he had hit something, so someone had to walk along to check the line.

Over the next two years I was called out many times for this job at all times of the night, searching the track with an oil handlamp and a torch. Sometimes I found nothing at all, other times a dead animal. I found seven human bodies in my time, persons who had committed suicide or wandered onto the track. If I found a body I marked its position on the sleepers with a piece of chalk and moved it to the trackside. I told the signalman from the nearest phone that there was a human body and the track was now clear. He would send the police who would take away the body, and then I could go home to bed. There was no counselling in those days, it was just an unpleasant part of the job.

Sally and I had no electricity in our cottage and we had to get our drinking water from a pump about five yards from the back door. The lavatory was a pail about ten yards further on down the garden, making a cold trip on winter nights. We had a Rayburn stove and cooker which kept the cottage nice and warm. Electricity was installed after we had been there about a year. We were very happy there.

Here is a picture of Sally just learning to ride a bike at Bentley. She had never had a bike as a child, so she never knew how, before that!

A big job each year was to mow the grass off the sides of the embankments to reduce the chance of a stray spark from the engines setting them  on fire and spreading to the adjoining fields. We also had to dig two spade-widths either side of the track fence and a yard square around all telegraph poles, mile posts and gradient posts to help keep down the fire risk.

Such fires did happen at times which meant that the farmer had a claim against the railway. It was very hard work standing on a sloping bank using a scythe. The cut took about three weeks by which time aching legs were normal and I did not want much rocking to get to sleep each night.

Keeping the track clean and tidy was a pride for the gangs. There was also a small cash prize given each year to the best section. Money was hard earned in those days as the basic wage was certainly not rich pickings. We set snares to catch rabbits on the embankments and we would share the catch between us or sell them to our neighbours for a few pence.

During a Sunday work party, it was not unusual to lift out a mile of old track and replace it with new, working nine or ten hours. There was a lot of maintenance work being carried out on the railway as the non-essential maintenance had been neglected during the war years. (Later, the new track-laying machines were coming into operation which did away with most of the pick and shovel work and meant that the track could be laid much quicker.)

We were at Thorpe-le-Soken, towards Clacton, when a nasty accident happened. We were loading rails by hand into "Longblues", special wagons that were 65 feet long to carry the 60 foot rails. Oh, and they were blue!

It takes 22 men to lift a 60 foot rail and load it into a wagon. You all bend down, pick the rail up and bring it up to chest height, then you throw it into the wagon. Hey - Up - Go!

On this occasion the edge of the rail caught on the ring on a man's finger as we threw, and that caused enough hinderance to stop it going straight onto the wagon. Instead, it bounced on the edge and fell back and broke the legs of two of the men not far along from me. I was unhurt, and lucky again. ❖

After that incident the chief engineer, Mr Baker, forbade anyone from wearing rings whilst rail loading. Those two men never did come to work again on the Sundays as I believe they were given light duty jobs in the office.

As a lad, Stan used to smoke a weed that grew around the hedgerows that we called Monkey Tobacco. He'd rub up the leaves to make it look like tobacco, and steal some cigarette papers from Dad to make cigarettes. It tasted pretty foul and I never got into that.

I started smoking a lot in the RAF, however, and I had been on 20 cigs a day and an ounce of Balkan Sobranie tobacco in my pipe. I gave up on November 10th, 1947 at half-past ten in the morning. I was recessing sleepers to take the screws at the crossing at Bentley, when I started to cough. This caused me to run the chisel into my left thigh where I needed three stitches. I said, "If that's what smoking does, I'll pack it up!" The other fellows, all puff-puff-puffing away, jeered at me, "You'll never pack it in!" But I did, and I never smoked another one.

We had the bad fogs and smogs in 1948-49 so you could not see across the width of two tracks. Everyone had coal fires in those days, making a dense smog of soot and smoke as the weather conditions didn't allow it to clear.

If the distant signal was yellow against the train, we had to put a fog detonator on the line to warn the driver, and also hold up an orange light for him as the signal light was twenty feet up and could easily be obscured by the smog. We had a brazier-type fire to keep warm (and add to the smog!) and a sentry hut in which to sit.

A fog detonator was a small explosive device about 2 inches diameter, 3/8ths of an inch high, joined to a piece of lead long enough to be folded round to clip it to the rail. When the train wheel went over it, the pressure caused it to explode with a noise loud enough to be heard over the engine, so the driver knew there was trouble ahead even if he could not see the signals in the fog, and could come to a halt. Sometimes pieces of shrapnel from the casing flew out and that could be quite nasty if you were nearby.

Self at Railway Cottages, Bentley

They were supposed not to be set off by impact, only pressure. However, Stan found out that was not the case when he was a boy of twelve. He was collecting coal off the railway for Granny. Odd lumps used to fall off the tenders onto the tracks, and kids would go and collect these up in a sack. This was trespass, and probably stealing from the railway, but I suppose a lot of people had to do it when times were hard.

As he went along he found a fog detonator that had been dropped. He didn't know what it was, but wanted to find out. He shook it, and could hear a rattle, and wanted to know what was inside. With his chum, Bill Ward, he found a big flint stone and whacked it to try to break it open on the top of Wherstead bridge. It exploded with a hell of a bang, gave them a fright and Stan had powder burns on his face and fewer eyebrows than usual. He was lucky not to be blinded.

We had one guard, Jim Cobbold, who was machine-gunned by German fighter planes when he was coming down Haughley Bank to Stowmarket. In the late 1940s, Peter Butcher was a porter who helped with the shunting at Bentley. He had found twenty out of date fog detonators and for a joke he placed them along the siding about a foot apart. Poor old Jim's train was coming in off the Hadleigh Branch line, and he was running off the wagons into the siding and was in the brake van, ready to apply the brakes to bring them to a halt.

When his wagons ran over all these detonators, he thought he was being machine-gunned again! He was so shocked he didn't put the brake on and the train ran hard into the stoppers, broke right through it and the wagons ended up on the footpath next to my cottage. Butcher was lucky to get away with that, and if it wasn't for Mr Parker he would have got the sack.

Butcher was a terror, actually. There was a chap killed near our road crossing who had his head cut off on the line. They put his body in the lockup at the station. I was off doing my garden that morning, and Peter sauntered over with the severed head tucked under his arm, and said "He won't sleep much tonight, will he?"

We used to have bucket toilets, and every year the railway would give us a new pail, as they deteriorated over time with the output my body produced! The 08:20 from Colchester came in and the passengers were about to board, when Peter held up my new bucket and shouted at the top of his voice to me up on the bank. Everyone on the platform and the train could hear his words, "Ivan! Your new shit pail has arrived!"

The women of Bentley thought a lot of him, though. He could not go in the services because he had very bad shakes, St Vitus dance they called it, but he would do repairs and things for the ladies during the war, like bolting in washers to fix holes in kettles and tin baths and so on.

Bentley was quite a busy little junction on account of the Hadleigh branch, a single line running through Capel St Mary and Raydon Wood.

When the Royal train came down from Sandringham, via Norwich, they would stay the night there. The train would stop to be reversed up the track there for the night with a police guard.

Normally the signalman would pull a lever to change the point, and then pull a second lever for the locking bar to keep it tight in place. This was usually enough, but when the Royal train was in, with a policeman by your side, you had to manually clamp the point on the ground to make sure it could not move when the train was going over it. We had the train in four or five times when I was at Bentley. It used to go up the line a mile and a half overnight, behind Bentley Hall. Then it would come out in the morning after the half-past eight train to London. We could see the Queen sitting in there with the Duke of Edinburgh having her breakfast and reading the paper. The Royals didn't have a special engine on their train, just any old one. Perhaps they washed it a bit first, though!

In 1950 a Class 4 Shunter job came up at Mistley, which was a bit more money at £4-8 a week, so I biked the six miles from Bentley to Mistley and back, six days a week, for those extra four shillings.

The station staff there consisted of a station master, two goods clerks, a goods foreman, goods porter and a shunter. Down on the quay was a foreman, tractor driver and a goods porter. There were also three signalmen and two platform staff. It was a busy place, more so during the barley season when it was not unusual to load forty or fifty wagons of malt barley each day. Then all the staff pitched in doing an extra four hours overtime, as all the open wagons had to be double-sheeted with tarpaulin for the long journey up to distilleries in Scotland.

The track from the upper yard down to the quay was about a hundred yards long and had to be descended with great care as it sloped about thirty degrees. There were no proper buffers at the end, just an upturned sleeper with the rails turned up. (This was because that line was supposed to be extended onwards, off through Mistley Heath to Kirby Cross and Walton, but the line was never completed. That's also why there is a brick bridge near the Wrabness road for no apparent reason. The cutting and embankments that had been started became a tank trap against enemy invasion in the war.)

A special brake van was kept on the slope to assist in the descent of wagons (only ten at a time were allowed). One day I apparently failed to put the coupling on properly, so when I released the brake it separated. There was no way I could stop the wagons running away down the slope and they ran down at a good speed to the end of the line and all derailed. At the inquiry I was just given a caution as there was no proof that I was at fault. ♣

They had an Artesian well at the Edme malt works which was about 300 feet deep, they reckoned. On a very hot day, a chap we called "old buskins" for obvious reasons, needed some water to drink. I suggested he go draw some up from the well. This was so ice cold it upset his stomach and he went off work!

One morning the signalman came to work on a three-wheeled bicycle. I laughed at him, and said, "What do you want that old thing for! I last had one of those when I was five years old!" He said, "Try and ride this one, then!" I did, and promptly crashed into some concrete buffer stops, badly buckling the front wheel. It cost me two pounds for repairs so that was an expensive lesson not to show off.

One day I picked up a young jackdaw on the road, a beauty he was but with a broken beak following some mishap. I took him home and we stuck a plaster on his beak and fed him with bread and water. The beak healed up solid but was not straight, so he could only eat by picking things up leaning his head to the side.

When I went off to work he would sit on my handlebars for a mile or so and then I'd say, "Off you go, Jack!" and he'd fly back home and spend the day around Sally. On the way home I would give a shrill whistle and call "Come on, Jack! Come on, Jack!" and he would fly over and perch on my handlebars for the rest of the way home. He was a lovely fellow and always came when we called. He stayed with us just over a year, until the springtime when I suppose he saw some other jackdaws, as he flew off and we never saw him again.

After a year at Mistley I applied for a Class 3 shunter job in Ipswich. That was better money at five pounds fifteen shillings per week, although it was seven days shift work.

Ipswich had three main sections. The top yard, where I was to work for the next two and half years, dealt with all the incoming and outgoing goods trains. It had fourteen sets of rails to accept trains and to make up trains for departure. There was a lower yard of about ten sidings and a big warehouse for loading and unloading goods for the town and the surrounding areas. Then there was a track to the dock area which had its own shunting engine, a steam-powered tram which could be driven from either end, with cowcatchers to remove minor obstructions from the track (similar to Toby in the *Thomas the*

Tank Engine stories.) All the yards were very busy places, taking in and out about five hundred wagons per day.

For the train buffs, here is a list of the freight trains from midnight onwards:

1:30 Norwich.

2:05 to March with empty coal wagons

2:10 Yarmouth

3:10 Manningtree and Harwich

4:20 Bury St Edmunds and intermediate stations

5:10 Lowestoft

6:00 Felixstowe

7:10 Hadleigh and Bentley

7:15 Aldeburgh

9:10 Snape.

Then there was a break when all the mainlines were required for the passenger trains, but we still had odd trains coming in with freight from Goodmayes near London and Whitemoor near Peterborough, as well as local trains coming back with the empties. There was also a large flow of traffic to and from the lower yard.

In late afternoon, the freight traffic began to flow again. The Fish Train from Lowestoft and Yarmouth came in for remarshalling, before setting off for Bishopsgate in London. The fast freight from Ipswich lower yard to the north of England left at 7:10 pm then the 9:10 was to Templemills in London.

Incoming empty coal wagons from Chelmsford and Colchester, added to our own collected from outlying stations, made up a train of about seventy wagons for Peterborough which departed for the collieries in the north of England at 11.30 pm.

We were only allowed a half-hour break for a snack and a cup of tea during each shift. It was a very busy job and at the end of my shift I was always glad to get home to bed.

Shunting was a dangerous game, and there were numerous incidents over the years. The shunter's job involved going round with a shunting pole to couple up the wagons to make up the trains. For the simple chain couplings you put your pole over the buffer for leverage, lifted the chain and hooked it on the other wagon's hook. For the screw couplings, these were made of left- and right-handed

85

screws, so as the coupling spun round it would pull them in together. You could spin this with your pole, although that took a lot of practise. Some of them were a bugger, as they had got bent or needed some grease and would not move with the pole alone. You often had to do them up by hand, which meant going in between the wagons.

If you had a good driver, he might push the wagons up against the buffer stops in the siding, and hold them there whilst you hooked them up. If the wagons moved for any reason whilst you were in there that was always a worry. One day a train moved slightly as I worked on a coupling and my railway hat was crushed between the buffers. Another two or three inches and it would have been my head. ☘

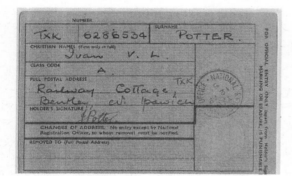

My National Identity Card 1951

We can't find any photos of me on the railways. So, I will have to make do with a 1965 holiday taken at Boscastle, on a holiday to Cornwall.

Chapter 14
On the railways, guarding the trains

A freight guard's job came up in 1953. That put my pay up to £6-2 a week. (My brother Stan became a freight guard too, a few years after me, so that's why I shall be mentioning him.) Being a railway guard was not easy. You had to learn every siding, every signal, every road crossing, every gradient, every bridge on dozens of routes covering hundreds of miles.

I had six weeks to learn the ropes, riding in the brake van with an experienced guard, learning all of those features in the whole of our area. This was quite an undertaking and led on to testing of my knowledge. My first trip was with a guard called Billy Hills, a real railway man who knew his job backwards, and a wonderful man who everybody liked. We rode from Ipswich to Whitemoor, the main East Anglian marshalling yard just the other side of March in Cambridgeshire, which had eight reception lines and forty-three departure lines and you had to know them all.

You had to prepare the train for departure, and were often using a shunter's pole to couple them up. You would tell the driver the details of the load, then you got into the brake van at the rear of the train and waited for the departure signal. Then you would lean out of the side of the brake van and hand signal to the driver on the engine that the train was complete, as in those days nearly all freight trains consisted of loose coupled wagons, not braked throughout. This meant that the engine could leave part of the train behind without knowing it, should the train divide. It was the fireman's job to occasionally look to the rear to make sure that the train was still complete. There were two forward-facing white lights on the brake van for this purpose.

There was a journal we had to fill in, on a specially printed sheet for each route. This consisted of the driver's name, guard's name, engine number, number of wagons and the total tonnage. The route was pre-marked on which we had to record any incidents, delays at yellow lights or reds and the reasons, or where you were directed into sidings to allow passenger and other faster trains to pass. This journal had to be handed in on arrival at the other end, or in the case of longer runs like Norwich to London, often the guard would change at Ipswich and the journal would need to be completed at that station ready to hand on to the other guard. A guard had to have a pocket watch to fill the times in, and it came as part of the uniform. It was a good one too, costing about £50 back in those days. (I had two and sold them in London after I retired, and they fetched over £100 each.)

The brake van was a box on wheels with a verandah at each end, a small coal burning stove, and a seat either side with a small slotted window from which one could look and see along the side of the train ahead. It had a large locker in which emergency equipment was kept, such as tow ropes and braking equipment. It had three oil lamps: one each side, almost at roof level, with a white light facing forward and red facing backwards. The third, tail lamp was in the centre of the van facing backwards. This told the signalman in the signal box that the train had passed by complete. This is the only time when a red light is an all clear signal on the railways.

After my six weeks learning the road with various other guards I passed my exam and was a fully-fledged guard. The guards job was always interesting as I went somewhere different each week and got to meet guards and staff from other depots.

A passenger guard had an easier job, in terms of knowledge, and could not work freight. Goods guards like us were qualified to do passenger trains as well, however, so we could not understand why we only got paid the same as them. Whenever we could, we would work a freight train into London and then cross the junctions and get to Liverpool Street, and be the guard for the passenger train back to Ipswich. That way we were working a shift and being paid rather than just riding back home.

The favourite job that both Stan and I tried to get was the 5:45pm passenger from London to Norwich. There was a millionaire jeweller or diamond merchant who got off at Marks Tey outside Colchester, then caught the train up to Sudbury. He was a lovely bloke but was fairly drunk most afternoons, and would often sit back with the guard. He had pockets full of miniature whisky, and if he struggled to open them he would tip us generously to open them for him, and also tip us for waking him up and help him stagger onto the platform for the Sudbury train! These extra tips always came in handy on our meagre wages.

There were 36 freight guards and 24 passenger guards based at Ipswich. We had round-the-clock duty shifts. My first job was in daylight, working a coal train round to the local coal yard at Derby Road near Ipswich. We had to shunt out the empty wagons and replace them with full brick and other goods wagons for unloading, and all this took about three hours. Then we had to go a mile along the line to Ransomes, Sims and Jefferies to take out their wagons loaded with newly-manufactured farm machinery. We would then attach the empty coal wagons and return to Ipswich, and this all had to be done between the times of the passenger trains running between Ipswich and Felixstowe. I did this job for a week, then moved on to another job for the next. With 36 guards in the gang we enjoyed quite a variety of jobs and destinations in rotation. The furthest point was Whitemoor which took between eight and ten hours to go there and back.

We also had "spare turns" on every shift, where one guard would wait in the local guardroom for a job, in case someone booked in sick at the last minute or needed replacing. You might just sit there for eight hours in case something came up. It often did, and even if you had already waited seven hours, you had to do that whole trip to see it through, so you might end up with a lot of overtime as well. A train could go nowhere without a guard.

It may be hard to imagine the noise in the big yards in those days across the numerous different tracks with the shunting engines, the locomotives and loads of wagons being banged into each other everywhere. If you heard a noise, you wouldn't know if it was your train or the next one. I certainly didn't hear one coming, one day, in Cambridge yard. I was sorting out the freight wagons and tallying the weights ready to depart for Ipswich. There were spaces between them, as the engine was not yet on and they had not been closed up. As I was walking along on the sleeper ends, they shunted some more wagons onto my train, which bumped the ones behind me and struck me a glancing blow in the back. The force threw me right over, but away from the wagons and track. If I had tipped the other way it would have been very serious. ❧

As it was, I was hurt and badly shaken up. The shunters helped me along to the inspector who, being a St John's Ambulance man, examined my badly grazed back, but reckoned I was still able to work my train back to Ipswich. After signing off duty I went to hospital for a check-up. I had a badly bruised kidney which caused me to pass dark urine for weeks, and they still keep an eye on my kidneys today.

Another night when I was preparing a train, I asked my engine driver to shove the wagons back on the buffer stops so I could couple them up. I was to signal him when I was done, by waving my oil lamps before putting them up on my van. I had to go in between to do up a stiff and awkward screw coupling that I had to do by hand. Just at that time a train arrived into the next siding, and a shunter went out with his white light to pull the train up from the stop point. He waved his lamp from side to side to call it up, and my driver thought that must be me saying I was ready, and he eased away.

The wagons that had been pushed hard on the buffer stops all sprung away and started moving apart. I fell down backwards between the rails, and the wagons went safely over the top of me. ❧ When he realised what he had done, the driver almost passed out with shock, and had to be relieved and sent home by taxi and he was off work for days.

One of the very first things I was asked when going on the railways was, "What's the difference between four foot and six foot?" The answer, they told me, is "Death". The distance between the rails is four feet (actually 4' 8.5") and the distance between two sets of tracks is six feet. If you lay in the "six foot" you are usually safe. (You could not stand there safely, of course, as the wind turbulence from a passing train might well knock you over.) If you are lying in the "four foot" you are not safe at all, as you are likely to be hit in the head by a coupling hanging down or a cow catcher. Of course, for a slow-moving train like the one that went over me, that was not a problem that night.

Not everyone had lucky escapes. I saw some very nasty accidents, like the crane operator who had got off his train to go and make a cup of tea. When he saw his train departing he ran across to jump on his crane, missed his footing and lost both his legs under the wheels.

Probably the worst one was at Ipswich in the mid-1950s when we were returning from a night engineering job. The Easterling train used to run non-stop from Norwich to Liverpool Street in London. It carried sufficient coal on the tender, 10 tons or something, but the water was used up quicker than coal and there was not enough on board. They solved this problem in a clever way. They put metal troughs between the tracks, about 70 or 80 yards long, which were filled with water about nine inches deep. When the express came along to that location, the fireman would lower a scoop from the tender and the water would be forced up the scoop to fill up the water tank. The Easterling did not run for long after the war, when the express trains began to always stop at Ipswich. They decided to remove the scoops from the main lines, so we had been out that night picking up the old water troughs from the Norwich side of Ipswich.

We were on the main Felixstowe line, waiting at a signal to back our train into Ipswich yard. There was a passenger train due to pass through before they let us across the other main line into the sidings.

At the signal where I was waiting there was a "dod", a round ground signal which is about 18 inches wide with a black strip across it. If it is horizontal it means danger, but when oblique it is safe. All the signals had oil lamps inside to illuminate them at night. The local lamp man was cleaning the lamp, bending down to wipe the glass clear and put a new wick in.

It seems he didn't realise there was a train due from Felixstowe. I was on the other side of my verandah when I saw the two-carriage railcar come under Hadleigh Road bridge about 70 yards away at 50mph or more. There was not enough time to move around to the other side and shout out a warning for him to squeeze up or lie down. The train hit him and knocked him ten yards back. He had lost the top half of his head and he didn't seem to have a whole bone in his body. It took six of us to pick him up by his clothes to put him on the stretcher. This was one of the ultimate hazards of working on the railway where one had to be on the lookout all the time for other traffic movements.

FLY SHUNTING

N.B. We usually had an 0-6-0 loco with six wheel tender, but for ease of illustration we show an engine without a tender.

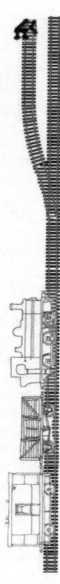

Step 1. Train heading for the siding, stops fifty yards out. Fireman dismounts and goes to man the points lever.
The guard dismounts with shunting pole, and stands alongside wagon.
The train moves forward, then brakes gently, allowing the guard running alongside to uncouple the wagons from the engine.

Step 2. With the engine uncoupled, the driver sets the engine to full speed, whilst the wagons carry on under their own momentum. As his brake van goes by, the guard jumps on to man the brake. As soon as the engine passes the points on the line, the fireman switches the points for the siding before the wagons arrive.

Step 3. The engine comes to a halt on the line. The wagons carry on up the siding as the guard applies the brakes to bring them to a halt.

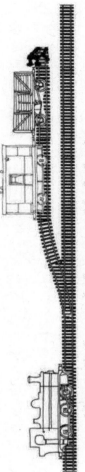

Step 4. The fireman switches the points to allow the engine to come back to the other side, and switches the points back to the siding again.
Meanwhile the guard uncouples the wagon(s) to be left in the siding from the brake van.

Step 5. The driver takes the engine up the siding to the brake van. The guard couples the brake van to the engine and boards.

Step 6. The driver takes the engine and brake van back onto the line, leaving the wagon in the siding.
The fireman sets the points back to the line and boards.
The train then returns from where it came, with the engine running backwards.

At times we had to do fly shunting, or what we called running off, usually on single track branch lines. This was a tricky and dangerous process to get a wagon into a siding under its own momentum, when the engine was facing in the same direction as the points went into the siding, but obviously you could not take the engine in ahead of the wagons. So, what you would do is take a little run up. The fireman would stand at the points. The guard with his shunting pole would stand alongside the wagon that was to be disconnected from the train and be put in the siding. The driver would pull away slowly, and when the train was moving he would apply the brakes for a second or two, to slacken the coupling, allowing the guard who was running alongside to use his pole to unhook the coupling of the moving wagons. As soon as it was decoupled, the engine would pull away fast, whilst the guard had to jump onto his brake van as it went past him. As soon as the engine crossed the points on the branch line, the fireman would switch the points into the siding, so by the time the wagons got to the points they would trundle in there under their own momentum. The guard, now back in the brake van, would screw the wheel down to put the brakes on and bring it to a halt. Then, the brake van would be uncoupled, the engine would go back through the points again and collect it out from the siding. They would then continue their journey or, where it was their last stop, would run back again from where they had come with the engine facing backwards.

My brother Stan was doing this one day on the Framlingham branch line from Wickham Market, which only took about one train a day. They had to leave one coal wagon at Marlesford station siding. Without running off, they would have to go all the way through Parham to Framlingham to be able to put the engine on the right end, and then come back again. They were not keen to do this, as that stretch of line had seven unmanned crossing gates. They would have to stop at each set of gates for the fireman to open them and hop back on, the train to draw through, and the guard to close them and get on again. All very time consuming, and they would have to do exactly the same procedure all over again on the way back.

Hence, they were doing this running off as usual, but when Stan came to leap on his brake van, it was wet with rain. His boots slipped on the step and he didn't make it on board. The coal wagon and brake van carried on without him at an increasing pace into the siding. Rather than the controlled braking that had been the plan, it came to a rapid halt at the buffer stops and a big shower of coal flew off the top of the wagon onto the road beyond.

Another time, Stan was collecting five empty coal wagons from a siding at Elmswell. These wagons had a heavy, six-foot square metal door that swung down onto a type of platform so they could be unloaded. They would have been emptied by hand by the coalmen, who would normally shut up the wagon doors when they had finished. It usually took two men to open and close them. Stan forgot to check they were all closed as usual... and they weren't! A bit further along on this siding was a series of parcel sheds on wooden pillars, a bit like Dutch barns, at the trackside. As the train drew away with all these metal doors sticking out on the horizontal, they sliced through a row of these pillars and the roofs were collapsing on the parcels and rats were running everywhere!

Felixstowe docks was rapidly expanding and taking all types of traffic in those days. At one time they were shipping a lot of cattle abroad in trains of fifty wagons containing eight or ten cattle each. After a while that livestock traffic was transferred to Brightlingsea in Essex. Then, for a year or so, there was a contract for train loads of motorcars from Coventry for export from Felixstowe.

I had the job of taking down the first nineteen modern shipping containers, which were unloaded by a mobile crane onto lorries, then driven on down to the ship. A far cry from today's way of dealing with them, with the trains going alongside the ships to be picked up by massive overhead cranes. Those early ships took only a small number of containers, where today they take thousands at a time on some of the biggest ships in the world.

One of the most unusual cargos we dealt with was bombs. This was when most of the wartime airfields had closed and all the unused bombs had to be disposed of. There were hundreds of trains of forty to fifty wagons loaded with bombs from the disused American airbases. These were loaded onto ships at Felixstowe and Cardiff and taken out to the Atlantic and dumped, which was deemed the best way to dispose of them.

On one memorable occasion I had to take a train of empty wagons to Elmswell to load up with bombs from the American airbase there. This was a long job as only six wagons could be loaded at a time, making a lot of shunting back and forth onto the main line to make up a fully loaded train of forty wagons. They were 1,000lb bombs, each about 4ft long and 1ft 3in diameter. A dozen were strapped down on each pallet, double-sheeted at the top and lifted into each wagon. I had to hang up all the couplings; there are three links on a coupling, and I carefully doubled them round to stop a hanging coupling hitting anything below to cause sparks or snags.

When the loading was complete, the train consisted of two standard steam engines with two armed American soldiers up front, 40 wagons of bombs, and then the brake van in which I rode with two more armed soldiers. These bombs were heading over to be loaded in Wales, and we had to take them as far as Cambridge. We were supposed to be given a clear road right though to Cambridge, but the gateman at Six Mile Bottom was late in closing the gates to road traffic, so the signal was against us. The drivers had to brake very sharply going down Dullingham bank, throwing both the soldiers and myself to the floor, causing several bruises and one solider to break his wrist.

As we approached Cambridge freight yard the train stopped. Looking out of my brake van I could see a number of railway staff looking anxiously around the front of the train, so I went up to see what was wrong. The sharp braking and momentum had caused quite a number of bombs to break loose from their straps and they had smashed through and were sticking out of the planking of the first five or six wagons! The whole area had to be closed off until the bomb squad came. It took nearly two whole days to make sure it was safe to move the train into the yard. That little lot could have blown up half of blinking Cambridge! ♣

Not so lucky were the brave men at Soham in June 1944. They were pulling a train containing 400 tons of bombs into Soham when they noticed the wagon nearest the engine had caught fire. Rather than legging it themselves, they decoupled all the other wagons and drove the train forward, and were in the station when there was a huge explosion which obliterated the station building. The driver was thrown a great distance and the fireman, who was trying to dowse the flames with buckets of water, was killed. They both got a George Cross, one posthumous of course, for their heroic actions. If the whole train had gone up where they had been, had they had abandoned it, the entire town might have been a crater. This tragedy was still being talked about on the railways for a long time.

I can't remember the details now, but I also heard tell of a railway man being injured where there was a derailment. The first wagon contained mustard gas and he got burned on the side of his face, but not fatally, and he may have been the only mustard gas casualty of the Second World War.

I took a packed lunch each day when I was a platelayer and shunter, but when I became a guard I did not take any food with me, and would have nothing on the eight or twelve hour shifts. I just didn't seem to need it, and I am still able to go for long periods without needing food. The only exception was in the 1987 gale. We were coming from Peterborough to Ipswich with a freightliner double-ended diesel. We got put into a siding at March when we couldn't go any further. I was with a young driver and we sat there waiting and waiting, until I went and asked the signalman what was going on. He said he had no idea how long we would be as there were no communications between March and Bury St Edmunds, and according to the radio, there was damage everywhere.

This was 07:45 in the morning, and we had started this trip back home at 06:45. It got to 11 am and I asked at the signal box again. He said they had comms with the controller of the area, but they are still not accepting any trains until the whole track has been examined. I said jokingly "Well, then, I think I will go and get fish and chips for lunch!" He replied, "The way things are going, I should buy your tea as well!"

The driver and I went and ate, and at 5pm we went into March again and got some more food; that was the only time I ate food as a guard. Our train finally left at about 8pm but only to Bury St Edmunds where we had to change over as we had been on duty so long. There was a bus service for passengers and crews onwards to Ipswich. It was 11pm the night before that I had started my shift, to 1am when I got home the following night. Sally didn't know where I was and was very worried, of course, but eventually she got through on a phone to the depot to find out I was okay. I put in expenses for the meals and overtime of 13.5 hours. And that was the easiest overtime I ever did, just waiting around and eating chips!

I met some real characters in my years on the railways. Jack Ashford was a guard, a tough old boy who lived at Whitton. His nickname was treacle as he was a real stickler. When he got his teeth into anything he would keep at it. At the beginning of the war he was a bargee from Ipswich to London. He told me they came back from London with a piece of teak they had salvaged from the River Thames, a 30-foot beam worth good money. They took it to Cranfields who wanted to use it but didn't want to pay for it, so he jumped over the desk and thumped the manager.

He used to keep pigs on his allotment and would go round all the houses in the area and collect the swill which he kept in a big, old enamel bath. His wife was as tough as him, and they were trying to herd a sow through from one sty to another with a piece of corrugated iron. This big pig charged at her and she jumped over the wall, but she landed right in the bath and was covered, head to toe. When Treacle finally stopped laughing he hosed her down with cold water.

In the guards' rooms, men from all over the area met for meals. Some London blokes were having their food there when Treacle played a prank one day. He stood up and was doubling over, saying "Oohh, I haven't half got a stomach ache! I can't hold this!" He dropped his trousers, and he squatted down. Behind him, Rex Roberts had popped a plastic turd on the floor, and poured some hot water on it, so it was steaming. When Jack stood up again, these London boys packed up their sandwiches and left double quick!

We set fire to the brick chimney at the guards' room in Ipswich one day. It was bitterly cold and the fire wouldn't draw. We had straw palliasses we packed around delicate items on wagons to protect them and stop them bashing into things. We took one of these and soaked it in paraffin and stuck it in the chimney. That roared up and the fire was drawing beautifully. Next thing we knew, the fire brigade appeared outside to deal with the huge flames shooting out from the chimney pot!

A guard called Jack Keeble was a funny old boy who couldn't do long journeys, so they just gave him short local trips. He would eat anything and everything, and would happily cook bacon on the back of a dirty shovel. If someone had not wanted all their sandwich they might put it in the rubbish. He would spot this and pick it up. "I'll take that home for the dog," he would mumble, as he slid it in his pocket. A while later his hand would go in the pocket and, sure enough, he would start eating it!

He came in one day and said "I got on to my missus this morning. I said to her 'That bowl of blancmange you left in the fridge! I ate it last night when I was hungry. It wasn't no good, you ain't put no sugar in it.' She said to me, 'That weren't blancmange, that was flour and water wallpaper paste I made up ready to do the papering this morning!'"

He was a rough old boy but he was very funny and could tell great stories, so they had him up the hospital to talk to people who wanted cheering up, or ones who might not make it through the night.

Another bloke used to do just one goods trip to Felixstowe, always the same route, to make it easier for him as he had broken his legs. He was writing out his journal, when Jack said to us, "Hold tight and watch this!" He set a penny cracker off under his legs, and the poor bloke nearly died from fright.

I was a passenger guard and ticket collector for the rest of my railway career, until I retired at the age of 65. I was proud to be the guard on the 12:50 from Ipswich to London when we carried Her Royal Highness Princess Margaret, the Queen's younger sister. She was accompanied by bodyguards and I had a policeman with me in my brake van.

One final word on the railways, and it will be a railways swear word. **Beeching!** They should have hung him at birth. It was a very worrying time when he was running amok, not knowing which lines would be shut next. He had shares in road building I believe and, in my view, he was a traitor to this country.

Chapter 15
Burning the candle at both ends

Times were hard and I always worked hard to get enough money in to keep me and the family comfortable. This meant I usually had more than one job on the go, and always kept an eye out for a bargain.

I had tried the life of crime in a very minor way when I was with the bad lads at RAF Swinderby, and decided it wasn't for me. I had actually been given a set of skeleton keys that opened any lock on the RAF station, which was how I got into the locked store room when I was after those maps. The shapes on the ends of keys spelled "hoteld." They were ever so thin, but terribly strong. I learned a bit about using them from the man who gave me them, who must have been a cat burglar in a past life! If you wanted anything, you'd just say, and he could get it. When I got demobbed I daren't bring those keys home so I threw them in the River Nene.

My life of crime was ended and I was straight as a die from when I went on the railways. Everything I wanted I paid for and (almost!) everything that made its way home from work was properly paid for.

I bought fifty coils of copper telephone wires when they were made redundant. I sold some of them to the maintenance builder on the railway crossing cottages who said they were ideal for bending to hold the slates on the roofs. The rest gradually got used for fences or were sold and I made a good profit on them.

There were miles of point rods being disposed of. They were the round type that ran on five-inch grooved wheels in racks. These went all the way from the signal box along the ground, 75 or 100 yards away, to alter the points. They did away with these round ones, and replaced them with n-shaped rods that ran over the top of solid wheels to reduce the chance of anything getting caught to stop them moving. I only needed three 25 foot rods, but the chance was there one day and I bought the whole lot on offer, a lorry load and a half, for just £25. Michael's neighbour immediately bought a lorry load to make a fence for his horses, so I made good money there.

When Sonia started school and Sally went to work at the fruit farm, this was good extra income that allowed us to buy a television set in 1951. I was the first working class person in the area to own a TV. It was a Bush 10 inch screen that I bought from Tooke and Vero in Ipswich for £110.

My dad and I erected an aerial which was forty feet high, using three of the old point rods. It was quite a task getting it up to this height. The people in the village could not believe I had bought my own TV, and said I had just put up the aerial for show! The picture was not always clear as there was an electric transformer on a pole quite near to the house which interfered with the reception.

During the Queen's coronation in 1953 we had over a dozen relatives and friends crowded into our lounge which was only eleven feet square. If anyone wanted to go to the loo all those at the back had to move to let them get out.

Another reason we could afford a television was all the extra work I did. Some jobs were more successful than others.

I met a chap called Francois Vandenbrook who was running a big old house as a hotel. He paid me to do odd jobs for him around the house and garden. At the time there were six coloured men from the West Indies staying there who worked at Cranes, a factory in Ipswich. They must have been amongst the first immigrants to come to work here after the war.

After a while Francois moved to Woodbridge to take over a second big house to run as a hotel. He asked me to go and help him in my spare time to decorate and build wardrobes and plumb in wash hand basins in all the bedrooms to make it ready to receive guests.

At the time, a large number of houses were being built on the two airbases of Sutton Heath and Bentwaters to be occupied by the Americans at the start of the Cold War. While they were being built, the families required somewhere to stay, which was a good opportunity for this new place. And then one of the officers suggested to Francois that he should apply to have a bakery on the base.

This was a big project and needed money, so my Dad and I each put up good our savings to help get it started. We bought an oven, dough mixing equipment, and a small Austin van in which to make deliveries. We had sole concession to deliver on both bases.

He made hundreds of doughnuts a day. Some filled with jam, others with crushed banana, all sorts. Americans certainly love their doughnuts! Francois and a chap from Martlesham were the bakers, coming in at 4:30 in the morning. When I was off duty from the railway I ran around on my Frances Barnett 197cc motorbike to help.

The profit on cake and confectionary is 66%. Francois made some money himself, and enough to pay the baker and young girl to do deliveries, but Dad and I had not been paid back or drawn any pay as yet.

Things were going quite well for about fifteen months until the firm American Delicatessens (the PX) realised the potential of the project. They had the capacity to deliver 1,000 items at a lift of a telephone. We could not compete with that, and when the bases did not renew our contract, we were left out on a limb. No money was coming in so Francois went bankrupt and both Dad and myself lost all our money. This was a bad blow to both of us, to lose all our savings that had been hard earned over a number of years. After a few months Francois emigrated to Swaziland and we lost touch.

Next, I tried to earn money with firewood and coal deliveries. Dad had already started doing that. He had stopped working as horseman at the farm due to some dispute with the farmer, and moved into forest work and became a warrener. Our family used to do all the rabbit control around.

Mick with Dad and the dogs
Jill and Nessie

Dad used to go ferreting on his own quite often, with his lovely mongrel, Jill, who was worth her weight in gold. He would put the net right over the holes in the bank then send her to guard the other side. The ferrets would go in and if they came out her side she would grab and hold them in the net. Dad stood on his side with his 12-bore shotgun. One time he saw a rabbit running under the net at the top and shot it, but in that split-second Jill

102

came over the bank and he killed her stone dead. He buried her there and came home absolutely in tears.

Dad would cord up tree-tops for Mr Parkin, a solid fuel merchant at Capel St Mary. Stan and I would help Dad in our spare time, as always. The trunks of the trees had been taken away for timber, leaving the tops to be disposed of. We cut up the branches into four-foot lengths, piling them into heaps four feet high and eight feet long, making the approximate weight of one ton. That is what is known as a cord, and for each one we made we were paid half a crown. All pieces under the size of your arm were put on a bonfire. The wood was taken to Mr Parkin's yard where it was cut up into logs for firewood and sold to the public.

I worked between railway shifts for Parkin, usually doing four or more extra hours a day. He had 11 customers when he started me on my round. When we finished up, I alone had found 311 of my own for my fortnightly rounds.

Jim Parkin had funny old Ford lorries. One was made in 1929 and his "modern one" was from 1932! We'd load the old one up with logs, and we would come through the middle of Ipswich. In the middle of the Cornhill or somewhere highly inconvenient, the gearstick would pop out and we would be desperately scrabbling to pop it back in so we could get out of everyone's way!

As the coal rounds got bigger and there were more customers in the surrounding villages, Mr Parkin bought two more lorries and hired drivers to cope with the extra work.

Things were going well, until I was caught out by the income tax people and they gave me a nasty sting. It turns out that one of my customers worked for the Inland Revenue and I suddenly got a letter stating that they knew I worked for Parkin and had not declared it. I went into the office. The chap said, "You have not been putting this work on your tax form."

"Oh no," I replied, slightly economical with the truth. "He doesn't really pay me, I help him out when he's busy in the winter and he gives me coal." He said, "That is still remuneration for services rendered, and it is taxable. Coal is worth so much a ton. I can prove you have worked for him for four years, because my chap has kept all the receipts you signed for him! Perhaps we can go even further back if we look into it a bit more?"

So, I was stuck. They took a third off my railway wages in back tax for two years, to compensate for what they said I owed. From then onwards Jim Parkin and the other coalmen made sure the tax man informant had not the tidiest delivery, with an unusually large amount of coal dust!

After that tax was paid, and I was financially hurting, I reckoned I could make more money by going on the coal round full time, so I left the railways.

I was coming back from East Bergholt, after delivering a couple of tons of coal at Randolph Churchill's place. That was when Stratford St Mary was still single carriageway on the steep hill, and the road from Higham joined the A12 on a steep slope. I was driving my lorry back along the A12 when suddenly, dead in front of me, twenty scaffold poles flew straight across the road and embedded themselves into the bank the other side. A lorry had come too fast down the slope from Higham and had had to brake hard which made the poles fly off his lorry. If I had been two lorry lengths further along they would have come straight through my cab, which doesn't bear thinking about. ♣

I did the coal job for twenty months until Easter in 1958, which was very cold so we had many more deliveries to make than expected. Jim asked, "How far will you get with your round today?" I said "How do I know? It depends on how it goes." He said "Well, I want to know. I want you to do things my way!" I was obviously not in a good mood, as I replied, "Well, if it ain't bloody good enough for you, I will leave!' He was in no better a mood than I, and snapped back, "Alright then!"

I had a delivery to make in Ipswich that same afternoon, so I went to the railway station with my coal gear on, saw the clerk Arthur Nicholls, and asked if I could have my job back on the railway. He said "Yes, but not as a guard. There is a job for a shunter." I gave Jim a fortnight's notice and started shunting for about four months until a guard's job came up for me, and there I was, back where I started.

Just before I went full time carting coal, my wife's Dad died, leaving her his bungalow in Bramford Lane, Ipswich. This was a great surprise to both of us as we thought it would be left to her brother Lionel. This location was much better for me, being nearer to my work at Ipswich station. It was a great property with fifty yards of garden, which was marvellous as I love growing vegetables and I had the space to build a large greenhouse for Sally in which to grow her beloved orchids.

In the early seventies with the help of my friend Michael Sawyer I built a dormer bedroom in the loft to make it better for our grandchildren to come and stay. I did all the electrics and the plastering, something of which I was very proud.

Chapter 16
My brothers, Stan and Mick

My two brothers were considerably younger than me, Ian (always known as Stan) was 10 years and Mick 16 years younger.

Stan in front of Charity Cottage, when it was still thatched. He had a headful of blond curls when he was a nipper. Our parent's window was the one seen on the top left. Mother was under the doctor and had some pills which caused her to hallucinate. In the night, she was crawling out of that window to try to catch an imaginary ferret. Dad had to grab hold of her legs to stop her falling out onto the path!

Below – Stan with Dad.

Stan left school at 14 and started work at Ransomes & Rapier on 1st January. That day was not a Bank Holiday then, it was just a normal working day. A basic working week was 48 hours, being 6 days including Saturday. It was not until the 1960s that they cut the hours when there was a shortage of work. He started his apprenticeship and didn't like it at all, being inside all day doing the same old thing. After three months he quit and went to work with Dad and Mr Gladding full time in the woods.

He knew he was going to be called up for National Service soon, so he volunteered for the army at 18, to get paid more. Conscripts got

paid 28 shillings a week, but regulars got 3 guineas. He chose the Royal Signals, as he wanted to be a dispatch rider, being motorbike mad the same as Michael.

As he went up in the trades learning radio, Morse code and so on, he got paid more. The military had their own way of training, whatever the job happened to be. They would normally take you out of your comfort zone to teach you the Army way. He trained at Catterick Camp and remembers crawling about on the Yorkshire moors with a radio on his back and a rifle in his hand.

Stan was extremely quick with maths. He was stationed at Woolwich and took the electric train to Whitehall every day. He had a female civilian boss from MI5 for whom he worked for about 18 months in London. Then he was posted down to GCHQ in Cheltenham where he was on the communications to places like Aden, Australia, New Zealand and West Germany. As he worked on the teleprinters and cypher machines, he got to see a lot of secret coding and is still under secrecy regarding the content.

Stan met an extremely beautiful young girl in Cheltenham and they went out together. After a couple of weeks his CO called him in and said he couldn't see her any more. He had to pack her up as her parents were half Russian!

He volunteered for three years and, the way the system was, they only tended to promote national servicemen as they wouldn't have to pay extra for the stripe until the last six months of their service, so it worked out cheaper. If the regulars got a stripe, the army would have to pay for it straight away. So, Stan never got a stripe, but had the same jobs as corporals and sergeants. A lot of people don't realise that. If you were good enough you could earn a stripe in nine months, but you wouldn't be given it. He went to his CO to asked why he was doing the same job as these guys with stripes. He was dealing with

FLASH messages, top secret most important, but was only a signalman, and stayed that way. Had he got the promotions, he would have stayed in and made it a career. But they didn't promote him, so when it was time to leave, he went.

He was demobbed in the August of 1956 and was on the Royal Army Reserves for seven years, but was almost instantly called back for the Suez crisis. They were all mustered ready down on the South Coast but that blew over quickly before they got sent out there.

Stan and Mick playing in the River Stour. Stutton Point is in view behind

Stan talks quite posh! He says, "Grandmother Potter was a school teacher, and my father was quite well educated. She spoke well, and I thought I should speak correctly too, but no one was teaching me. I was saying, "Ahhr boy, what are yer doin?" and wanted to get rid of that Suffolk accent. I listened to the radio news readers like John Snagge, Stuart Hibberd and Alvar Liddell whenever I could, as I thought their accents sounded much nicer.

"When I was in the war office I was around Old School boys and I honed it there. Mother used to refer to me as her educated son, which I wasn't, but I could put myself over well when I wanted to and could mix in all circles. I have lost it a bit in my old age and now sound closer to my Suffolk farming roots again."

When Stan came out of the army he didn't know what he wanted to do. I went in the office at Ipswich and got him a job on the Railways. He started as a shunter, then guard, ticket collector, foreman at Felixstowe docks, then supervisor at Felixstowe and finally the top supervisor for East Anglia freight at Ipswich. Like me, there was never a day he didn't want to go to work. So, that was some job I found for him!

One night, Stan and I were watching ABA boxing on the television at my house in Railway Cottage, just 25 yards from Bentley railway station, when we heard an almighty crash that sounded like a train had crashed into the station.

In fact, the locking mechanism had failed on the road crossing, the signal had been green and the Up train had smashed through the gates travelling at seventy miles per hour. We ran down to the crossing where the gate porter stood in a state of complete shock. Seeing that the signals were still green for the Down train, I phoned the signalman and told him what had happened. We grabbed the porters handlamp and ran towards the oncoming train waving a red light. The driver saw this and was able to stop his train before reaching the station, which was littered with the smashed wooden gates. The engine we stopped was the famous Oliver Cromwell and the driver was Fred Flowers, based at Norwich.

By this time the station master had arrived and asked if Stan and I would search for debris fouling the track. Knowing where the tools were in the platelayers hut, we set off clearing up the pieces. When we were sure the track was clear we phoned back to the station from a phone on a signal, to allow the train to continue. The station master said that he would send in a report to head office about the help that we had given, and both Stan and myself were given two hours pay and a special commendation on our records.

Stan got married when he was 26 but his wife turned out to be an absolute b****. As he says, "From the minute I put the ring on her finger, I have never seen anyone change so totally like that." She got him in debt left, right and centre. It was not a happy marriage and it all went wrong.

When their daughter was about three and their son was a baby, he was working at Parkeston as a guard on a night train, when he got an urgent message from the police, saying "Your baby son is home alone in his cot, and your wife is not there." I am not sure if the wife took her daughter with her that night, or if my niece wandered out and the police found her. What we did know was the wife had gone off with Stan's best friend, another guard called Brian. Stan and Brian used to spend a lot of leisure time together. Brian worked a different shift, so whilst Stan was at work he had been carrying on with the wife. Anyway, Stan went home to Holly Lane in Belstead and met the police there with his children. We had to stop those two men meeting up at work as we worried that Stan might kill him!

The wife left Stan and took the children with her. For the next twelve years, whenever Stan earned anything over £20 a week the government took every penny of it out of his pay before he saw it. He did not really see his kids again. I think she turned them against him, and they would not even ask him to their weddings. Stan now has two daughters, in theory, as his son had a sex change at 21. He came out looking very good, and at the time you'd have no idea he was once a boy!

Stan was tough and strong like Dad. As he says, "If you swing a seven-pound axe all day, you build it up without knowing it. I had a 26" waist and 42" chest. I could shove nails through wood, with just a piece of cloth to protect my palm, and crack walnuts in my elbow."

One day at work on the railway, he was lifted up by his hair for a £5 bet. They sat him on a chair and he held on to the bottom, they got hold of his hair and lifted him right up, and he won.

Stan was mad keen on karate and judo, and was a black belt, chopping broom handles in half, and the like. He had big trouble with his knee after one Judo competition. He threw a 16-stone man and it didn't go as planned, as the bloke fell on Stan and caused his leg to be bent up badly behind his back. He went for convalescence at Felixstowe, where Sally and I went to visit him. There was a beautiful red-headed woman walking the ward. He said. "See that nurse over there? I'm going to marry her."

"Oh really? What's her name?"

"Well, I haven't got that, yet!"

Her name turned out to be Joyce Harrison, and within three months they were going steady together and got married. She had also been married before, with a son and a daughter who stayed with her and Stan got on fine with them.

110

Stan and Joyce when they got married. Joyce didn't like her picture being taken, so there are few of her to choose from

Stan was in a financial muddle thanks to his first wife but Joyce took every pay packet, took the money out for house-keeping and paid off part of his debts each week, and soon got him into order with not a lot of pocket money!

When they first dated, Stan said something like "...as long as you don't like dancing!" She didn't say anything and covered up the fact she was a very good dancer, actually No. 4 in the world or something. One day, after they had been married a while, a man came to the door and asked her to fill in for his sick partner. She agreed to help and went out. Stan was most shocked about it, but when he found out she was one of the top ladies he decided he should learn to dance himself.

They became dance champions together and won 68 champions, including finals in Paris and Denmark, and have loads of trophies. After he stopped ballroom dancing, Stan became an adjudicator.

After 45 years of wonderful marriage, doing everything together, Joyce died in 2012. In her memory, he sponsors the Joyce Potter Celebration Cup at the Felixstowe Dance Festival. Stan felt his life was finished, but had to keep busy. He took up golf, and after a bad winter prevented much golf from being played, he took up snooker as well. He paints pictures, like me, and does fly fishing and he "makes and crashes powered model aircraft".

He says, "I have had a terrific life, I would not change anything, even the worst parts, as they are what made me. Nowadays I am so laid back and agree with people, even when I don't. Rather than confront people and thump them, why not just get on with it?"

On to our younger brother Michael, who has always been motorcycle mad. When he finished at Copdock school, aged 15, he went to Revetts Motorcycles in Ipswich, a dream job for him working with his main passion in life. He did his first scrambling race on his

16th birthday at Burstall. This was the start of a long career in scrambling and road racing of both solo and sidecar machines. He raced at the Isle of Man, in Ireland and on the continent, doing very well. He has won a pile of trophies and still does the odd veterans race and classic parades even now, in his late seventies.

Mick with his friend Frank Barber

Michael didn't learn to drive a car until he was 27. I used to drive him around to the races and watched and took photos. Stan drove him around to races as well, as he also loved bikes. I borrowed a bread van a few times in order to get his bike to race meets! After Mick could drive himself we all had our own lives and went our own ways a bit, and only got together again in more recent years.

Mick was called up for national service and didn't want to go in, as he would not be able to scramble. However, like Stan, he went in the Royal Signals, as he knew about their motorbikes.

He got into their White Helmets motorcycle display team, and being small and skinny, he was the top guy on the famous pyramid. He had only done a few shows when he got called to the office. His medical history had caught up with him. During the very cold winter of 1947, Mick was hospitalised with an ear problem. That was about the last time he has been in one! He had had a mastoid (ulcer) in his ear making him partially deaf, so they discharged him from the army. That broke his heart, now that he had got into the world famous display team. He loved the riding bit of course, but always loathed the military side. He didn't like the discipline at all and hated the way the NCOs treated the privates. But anyway, he was out on his ear (ha ha!) and went back to work at Revetts.

Now, in 2017, we learn the White Helmets will soon be disbanded. All of us brothers are very sad about that, losing one of the icons of this country.

Mick lives at Belstead and has his own scramble track and lets some local youngsters practise on it. The sport is called motocross these days. For his 60th birthday we hired the Village Hall at Belstead. All the fellows who he helped with racing over the years had a whip round, and presented him with a cheque for £2,100. When he was first handed it, he read it and thought it must be £210! He has an interesting old Triumph, where the top part of the engine came from the petrol generator starter motor for an Avro Lancaster. These were made by Triumph and it is still coloured RAF blue on the cylinder head.

I could write a book about Mick's life and fascinating career, which is everything motorcycles, but it is already being written. His book is in the early stages and will hopefully be out next year.

A Racing sidecar. Mick and a friend from Colchester built one of the first "kneelers", only 19 inches to the top of the steering column. This was a Vincent 1000 scramble sidecar outfit before they raced on the road. His dog is seen trying out the chair.

Chapter 17
Motor mad

W e three boys were all into motorbikes as youngsters, and then Stan and I got into cars for the most part. Mick still dislikes driving cars, it's only bikes for him.

Dad got a car, a 1934 Morris 10 with the accelerator in the middle, different to everything else! He had never driven anything mechanical in his life, but learned to drive that very quickly and passed first time. Both Stan and I learned to drive in that car. Stan passed his test just three weeks after his 17th birthday. He cleverly booked the test in Ipswich on Wednesday after early closing, when the shops shut down and not much traffic made it easier.

Mr Gladding was a great friend of the family. He lived next door to us in Charity Cottage, and was like a father to Mick after our Dad died. In the background is Dad's old Morris

Washbrook Garage was a little garage on the hill on the old A12 which came up for sale in 1947. We were all into vehicles and I was just out of the Air Force and was deciding on what to do. Dad was thinking of buying that for us three boys as he knew the owner well. We didn't buy it, and the owner carried on. His name was Bonner Wyatt and it was a bit alarming that he would serve petrol with his pipe burning! That garage became very big in classic motorcycles, and it was a later owner, Pete Easton, who started off the Copdock Motorcycle Show at the Village Hall a few hundred yards away. It has now become a huge annual event and had to move into the Suffolk Showground near Ipswich, but has still kept its local name.

I had a few motorcycles, being much cheaper than cars to buy and run. I had a Francis Barnett with a 197cc Villiers engine. In about 1950 I bought the first cycle-master that I saw on display in Mayhew's window on the Norwich Road. It was a little 50cc that was all built in to an enclosure on the back wheel. That had a back-pedal brake and it would stop on a sixpence. The third time I was on it I back-pedalled too hard and it put me over the handle bars.

It was about 1954 that I got my 250 BSA pre-war side-valve bike with a right-hand hand-change that did me well for several years.

I bought my first car in 1953, a Morris Oxford with the old rounded shape like the Minor. I got it on HP (hire purchase) for £300 from Washbrook Garage, as Bonner knew that he would get his money alright from one of Dad's family.

I have had about 16 cars in all. Only one was from new, an Austin Maxi that cost £1,375 and I did 113,000 miles in it. It was still going well when I sold it. I never had an engine pack up on me. Other cars included a Mini, a Princess, 1100, Morris traveller, MG ZR, Rover 25 and two VW Camper vans. Currently I drive a VW Golf.

I used to repair cars for people, servicing them and doing brakes and clutches. It was quite funny one time, when the assistant manager at work, Mr Graham, came to collect his car after I had replaced his brakes. He picked up the old brake shoes to look at them and got his hands dirty. I said, "You can go through there to wipe your hands, there is Swarfega and paper towels." I had not thought that both of those items happened to be "borrowed" railways issue, but he didn't say anything about it!

Apart from the donkey and the motorbike I only had one accident in my life. It was at Martlesham BT roundabout, where I misjudged the speed of a chap coming from my right. He was haring along to pick up his daughter and glanced my front. And I haven't been of interest to the police either, except for one little speeding ticket. I have been an AA member for 64 years. I talked them into knocking off another bit this year, saying I must be about their longest and oldest member still on the road! I call them 'my friends I don't want to talk to'.

Stan is very much into his cars. His first car was a big American Studebaker which he got because it pretty much had a double bed in the back! When "BBC 253" faded away he came down in the world a bit, with an Austin Seven. As soon as he could afford it, he bought a Jaguar, but he could only afford to get five bob's worth of petrol at a time. He would race it up and down Copdock Road. Mick would sit inside next to him and could read out that they got up to 105 mph, as Stan couldn't drive it that fast and also read the speedo! Now he has bought a BMW 740 limo with mainly 750 running gear, which cost £73,000 new but he picked it up second hand for just £3,000. It was the only one of its kind, like a transition prototype and goes like hell.

Above: Ivan, Michael and Stan   Below: Stan and his BMW

Chapter 18
Losing Dad, and Mother's secrets

We lost Dad quite young, in 1954, when Michael was still only a teenager. Dad was logging in Shrubland Park with a fellow named Alf Garnham, when Dad accidentally cut his foot. They had chain-sawed through a log, leaving a bit uncut at the bottom so the chain would not hit the soil and become blunt, then rolled it over for Dad to chop through the last bit with a big blow of his axe. It went through easier than he thought and carried on down into his foot. The axe blade cut right through this shoe and severed the top leaders of his toes. He jumped about and said "Gracious, look what I done!" (He never swore. The worst we ever heard out of him was a "Damn!") Mr Garnham whipped him into hospital where they sewed the top of his foot up. He was incapacitated for about a month before it got well enough for him to walk about.

Dad and Mr Garnham cutting down a tree

Not long after that, however, Dad got an ulcer in his stomach and went for an operation. Whilst in hospital he caught pneumonia. He coughed violently and busted his stitches inside, and that did for him. The day he died they put eight pints of blood in him whilst I sat there.

117

Stan was over in Cheltenham at that time, but his unit got a phone call from my mother, saying father hadn't got long to go. She said "I forbid him to come on his motorcycle, it is too dangerous, as he will

rush back too fast. Please put him on a train." So the CO called him in and arranged for him to be taken to Gloucester station, and Uncle Ted collected him from Ipswich Station.

Stan came in when I was sitting by Dad, who put his hand out and said, "You made it, boy. I'm glad you did," and within fifteen minutes he was dead. His last words were "Good luck, all on yer." Mick was at work with Revetts at the time, but he didn't like hospitals anyway and would not come in.

We all thought he had been the greatest man that ever lived.

Mum was rather unusual, as she was a white witch. She was very astute in country ways and there were a number of things that happened around her that were beyond our belief.

Michael built her a granny flat on their house. When she died in 1984 they found in her rooms a shoe box containing seven plasticine dolls with pins stuck in them. She would go round cursing people and the villagers were terrified, because if mother condemned them, a few days later it was inevitable something would happen to them. The old boy in the Post Office was on the Village Hall committee and he would not vote for her. They had a blazing row and mother said she would get him back for that. Three days later he fell off his bike and broke his arm.

When Mick's first wife left home for another man who was his business partner, she said to him "Your business from now on will go downhill, and you will never profit from it." Within a year that was the case.

Dad's half-brother Ted (Edwin) was unmarried and my mother had carried on with him for years. Dad wasn't a church-goer and nor was Mum. She went anyway, but it turns out it was through the woods to Bentley Church, and the purpose was to meet up with Ted!

Mum and Ted got married not very long after Dad had died. I refused to go to the wedding as I hated him for it. Stan accepted it, but didn't go to wedding as he was away in the Army. (The keen reader might have spotted that Stan has Edwin as a middle name.) Mick would have been riding or fixing a motorcycle, no doubt, so he didn't go either.

My brothers have a different view of our mother than I did, and they remember her much more fondly. Stan says, "She had a bloody hard life, working on the farm, bringing up three of us, and we weren't the easiest of boys. For instance, there were two boys who also worked in the woods with their Dad, also in their early teens, and Mick and I took them on with proper air rifles. We had battles shooting at each other! We were quite safety conscious, mind you, as we had a rule: Don't shoot no faces, only body parts.

"In those days the man was out at work all the time and the woman had to do all the discipline, which Mum did and she kept us in good order. The youngsters today could do with plenty of that which would sort out many a problem. Yes, she was a bit harsh at times, but she was a good mother, I remember when I was aged about 8 being bullied by some evacuees, and she went and sorted that out right away with a few choice whacks!"

Mother with Stan and baby Michael, and Floss the dog

Mick adds, "Ivan was much older than us, and of course she was younger too at that time, so her arm would be stronger. Perhaps he got beaten a bit harder than us, and his bum remembers it more! Who knows?"

Anyway, Stan and Mick both say they would not have swapped our mother for anyone.

The funny thing is that mother had long planned for her burial to have a glass-top coffin, so when she was put in the ground, the last thing we three boys would see was her. I refused to follow that plan!

Poor Uncle Stan died young in 1958. He had just retired from the police and still lived in Hounslow with his wife and family. He took his car in for a service and the mechanic said, "Sorry Stan, I can't give you a lift, but you can borrow this moped to get home." He headed off on that, when a lorry came out of a side road and ran right over him. He had done all the time during the blitz of London and survived, and there he was dead from just a careless driver.

Chapter 19
Fishing and other pastimes

I always loved gardening, and still do. I also love fish! When we moved to Bramford Lane in 1958 we dug a large double fish pond, and wanted a bridge to go between them. That structure needed some reinforcing, so that was the most useful end of my Hopper bicycle of which I had been so proud.

My bridge in snow   *Holding Scamp and Yogi*

We kept various breeds of dogs for many years and most of all I adored Yorkshire terriers. Scamp weighed only 4lb and Yogi Bear was 6.5lb. When I went shopping with Sally, and Scamp was a pup, he would sit in my pocket under my arm. All the ladies would stop and coo over him. I rather wished I'd had him when I was about 20!

When we first came to Bramford Lane, the butcher at Ulster Avenue noticed I was new and we soon got talking. I told him I loved beach fishing and he said "Really? My son-in-law is just around the corner from you and he's looking for a fishing partner." He gave me the details.

I went round to Diamond Close and rang the doorbell. When this smashing bit of stuff opened the door, I thought to myself, "Good God, this is no good. If that's his missus, he certainly won't be leaving *her* just to go fishing!"

I was wrong, and Russel Mexome became my longest and best friend and we fished together for years. (He has sadly got bone cancer now; his wife, Peggy, is still just as lovely.)

Russell was an engineer at *East Anglian Daily Times* when they sent him to Birmingham on some printing course, and whilst he was there he went to night school to learn about fibre-glassing. He announced to me, "We are going to make a boat ourselves!"

He had a little pram dinghy which we turned upside down, then extended it with hardboard from eight feet to fourteen feet. We covered that with cling-film to make the male former. It took thirteen hours one Saturday to put six layers of fibre-glass all over it.

The next weekend we took our boat off the mould. We used lots more fibre glass to make two boxes in the stern for buoyancy, put a seat in the middle with buoyance boxes, and at the bow we filled in another buoyancy section to made it more unsinkable than the *Titanic*. We set a piece of wood around the gunwale and installed a little Anzani outboard engine. We launched it, with the name *Wimadit* - you guessed it, we made it!

Some very nice catches of cod

The Anzani was only five horsepower, making it suitable for going up to a mile offshore. One day we had drifted out two miles when we found the damn thing would not start, and it took us an hour to row back against the tide with one oar each. It was such hard work we decided to upgrade to a new 50hp Mercury motor.

We kept that boat for about ten years, mainly fishing off Felixstowe. We would go out three-and-a-half miles to Cork Lightship where we would drop anchor at the little shelf out there in about forty feet of water.

One day we launched opposite the Fludyers Pub in Felixstowe and had been out fishing when it got a bit too rough. When we came in, one of us would control the engine whilst the other jumped out the bow. I jumped out and found it was deeper than I thought. My feet and knees sank into the shingle and I got properly stuck! I wore a life jacket, but I could not move and the waves were lapping over my head so Russell had to pull me out by my hair! ❧

It was a firm rule of mine that we always wore life-jackets. I had a friend called Tommy Charlton, who'd done six years in the Navy including time on the Murmansk Convoys. I asked him to go fishing, and handed him a life jacket. He scoffed, "I am not putting that bloody thing on, *I've* been in the Navy!"

I said, "Tommy, I can only just swim. If you fall out and go unconscious, what am I going to tell your wife the next day?" He could see my point and I had no trouble after that. We had many good catches together.

It was true that I was not a good swimmer. At Stutton shore we never thought about swimming, we just paddled about with toy boats and things. Mother did swim there, but she preferred to catch flat fish. At low tide she would go to Holbrook Creek where she would feel them under her feet, then fling them out.

In the RAF we did dinghy drills in a pool, to demonstrate that we could swim, which in all honesty I couldn't.

Stan & Mick with a toy yacht at Stutton shore

I had to jump off a 15-foot high diving board with all my flying gear on, make my way to the dinghy and turn it over, and then climb in. (The buggers always set it the wrong way up on purpose.) I was struggling in the water as, to make things worse, my Mae West punctured when I jumped, and only the kapok within was keeping me afloat.

I was swimming around and this Corporal could see I was not so good, and he had got a pole with a rescue ring on. He held it in front of me saying, "Go on, catch onto this!" But he kept moving it ahead of me until he had taken me 25 yards of this bloody pool. If I had just thought about it, in my panic, I could have put my hand out and grabbed the side! I could have whacked him at the time, but I thanked him later, as it taught me I could swim with the full gear on and it was good to know I could save my life with swimming.

There was a strange thing one day when I took a friend from Felixstowe out to Cork. We suddenly saw a thick sea fog coming in, so I turned us back. We came back on the compass as usual, and about 100 yards from shore I looked on this compass and we'd

A nice garfish, just one ounce under the record

apparently gone in a circle. It didn't seem right, as I could see the waves were breaking away, so we carried on as we were and landed safely. We told of this in the pub and other people said they had had funny compass readings as well. The only solution we could come up with was that someone had lost a large outboard motor or something overboard, and the compass was picking up its magnetic field.

I loved my sea fishing in that boat. I went with Russell until my shifts no longer worked in with his leisure times. I bought his half of the boat and eventually I sold it altogether, as I had no one else to go with. I did go for many other boat trips and plenty of beach fishing on my holidays.

124

Sally liked fish, but not the water. She would happily swim in the river, but didn't like the open water at all. Even on the big ferry we took to Holland for a weekend, she wouldn't go and look over the side!

"Ivan Thrower" in his greenhouse and Judy the mongrel

A skate that was fun to land   Fishing off some Cornish rocks

Chapter 20
Making things

Making and fixing things has always been a great love of mine. When we were kicking our heels so much in the parachute cloakroom, I made jewellery to sell, including snake bangles, rings and broaches with mounted stones.

One of my prides was the model of a Lancaster with a thirteen inch wingspan that I made at Swinderby out of window perspex, using just a file. A chap offered me 50 quid for it at the time, which was a lot back then.

The material for the main model came via my brother-in-law Nick, from the B17 that crashed at Framlingham. The square base came from the Wellington we crashed at Wing. A friend saw me afterwards and asked me, "Did you get a bit?" and when I said I hadn't, he said he'd saved me a piece, being part of my W/Op side window.

Unfortunately, Sally put the model on the front room window sill for a while, and the heat of the sun made it go milky, and that has spoiled it a bit. I have given it for display in the Martlesham Heath control tower museum, along with some other bits and pieces.

I have donated lots of bits here and there to various museums. An ex-RAF chap gave me two Wellington bomb release switch panels years ago. I gave them to a model railways enthusiast, who needed some switches to operate the points and signals on his layout. When he went digital, he offered them back to me. I donated one to Morton-in-Marsh and the other to Martlesham.

I have made a lot of things out of wood. I thought long and hard about setting up my own little business, called "Bits of Wood". I had a Nissen hut at Bentley, that I moved with us to Bramford Lane, and in it I always kept odds and ends of wood of all shapes and sizes. I was thinking about the number of people who wanted a small piece of wood for a job to match for a repair or for a project. People would come to ask me and I could usually help them find something from my stock of hardwood, timber, veneer, and ply. I didn't usually charge people, but noticed I seemed to be doing it often enough to make a business out of it.

Mum at my Nissen hut

When Michael was the foreman at Revetts they had packing cases of "bastard mahogany" that the Honda motorcycles were shipped in from Japan. He brought a lot of that wood home to burn in his log burner, but I would help myself from his big pile. I took good bits I thought were too good to burn and made a pretty coffee table.

A friend was doing some gardening for two elderly sisters. He mentioned they had asked him to chuck out two old mahogany beds. I said, "Don't do that!" I went along in my car and saved the end boards and sides. I joined the two ends into a big dining table with feet crafted from two old fashioned mirrors of the type that stood on dressing tables. I had salvaged these at a different time and reinforced them with steel rods inside them.

I made all sort of things in wood, such as a dolls house for my granddaughter, Michelle.

In 1955, at my home village of Belstead, about twenty people started a project to build a village hall. My mother was a key organiser. It was quite a task, and hardly any of us had any building skills. With supervision from those who had, we made a start, working mostly Saturday and Sunday mornings. The brickwork was supervised by a Mr Fayers who was a foreman building Ipswich power station at Cliff Quay and was in charge of the two massive brick towers. He would come over each Sunday morning to inspect our brickwork. Too often, to start with, he would say "That one ain't quite right" and he would make us take the rows off until we could get to the offending brick and set it right. When those walls came to be plastered on the inside, the plasterers said it was some of the best brickwork they had ever covered up.

When we got up to the correct height for the roof, the steelwork arrived. It had been made up for us by a firm in Ipswich so all we had to do was to assemble it, which we did with more determination than skill! Then the ten feet by four feet asbestos sheets arrived to cover the roof. As I was the youngest and most agile of the helpers that day, I was volunteered to go up to the top of the roof to haul the sheets up by rope. I was standing 25 feet up on the ridge where I held the sheets in place as they were drilled and bolted in.

This went well until I was hauling up the penultimate sheet, when the rope broke suddenly. I lost my balance as it gave way, and I fell from the top down the other side of the roof. Everyone came running round to the back of the building fearing the worst, but luckily I was only bruised. I had landed right on top of a heap of soft sand that had just been delivered, ready to plaster the inside walls. ❧

The next big job was to dig a large cesspit as the village was not on mains sewerage. One Saturday, whilst the other helpers took the earth away, Stan and I dug the hole by hand, 16 feet by 8 feet by 10 feet deep, down to the soft sand to let the liquids soak away, with the solids to be pumped out in due course.

We were very pleased with this work, with lovely straight sides. We left it, ready to concrete in a base on the Sunday morning. Of course, I went off to work on the railways after that day's leisure! I always did a lot of nights for the time-and-a-quarter pay. Some chaps didn't like to do nights so I did mutual swap-overs whenever I could.

With such long days and nights, I caught up sleep as and when with what they call a power nap nowadays. I might even manage a couple of hours on some easy shifts. I admit I did fall asleep a few times when I shouldn't have done. We guards trained ourselves to instantly notice if the train dropped speed, and would wake ourselves up. We were supposed to look out of the little side-view windows of the brake van, and if we spotted a signal the driver had missed, which was rare, the idea was to screw the brake on hard. The driver would soon feel that up his end and would brake the engine as well, and then come and find out what the guard had seen.

One night I woke up when the engine shut down at Willesdon, near Wembley, and I realised I had missed the whole journey across North London, all the way from Stratford!

The brake vans were done away with once the wagons were all close-coupled with vacuum brakes throughout. Then, the guard simply sat in the other end of the diesel cab. There was nothing to do or see to keep you busy, you just had to write down the times and stops. I would often sit up with driver if I could, just to keep awake. Paperwork used to be taken in at the destination for each wagon, but then they even got rid of that system, as it was lodged in a special compartment on each wagon so you didn't even have to deal with it. The shunter started to do all the work of building the train up and checking the brakes were working throughout, and off we would go. It became quite an easy job as a guard, and very different to when I first qualified.

Anyway, back to our hole! During that Saturday night when I was at work, there was a terrific thunder storm. All the rain ran down the slope of the road from Buck's Horns Lane into our lovely hole. We came back on Sunday morning to find a muddy pond with very collapsed sides. We were unable to do anything with it for three weekends, waiting for it to dry out, and as we dug it all out again we were wishing we had thought to use shuttering to shore up the sides.

129

The hall's floor was best Canadian pine, all laid with secret nailing. I was one of the ones doing that, as the number of helpers had dwindled somewhat by this time. In November 1961 the remaining ten of us finished the whole job.

The hall was opened by Lord Belstead on the 16th of December 1961 and we volunteers who had seen the job finished were given the freedom of the hall. This means that if we need the hall for a function we do not have to pay to use it. I used it for my daughter's wedding and again for my 90th birthday celebrations in March 2014.

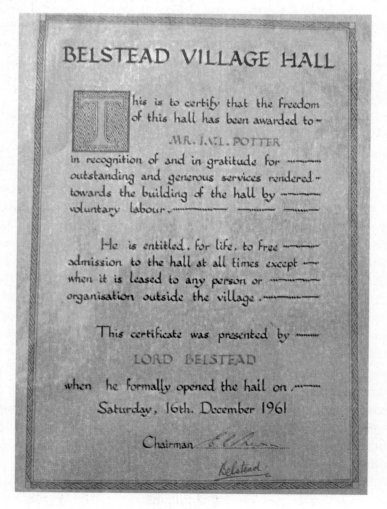

Photos I was given from the opening ceremony for the Hall. I am the handsome devil on the right, Ted and Mum are in the big picture as well

In my retirement I did a lot of modelling and oil painting. I am proud of my model of the *Cutty Sark* which is on display at Felixstowe Maritime Museum and may next go to the new Woodbridge Museum.

At work in my garage studio making the finished article

Oil paintings of a fishing boat I went on, and a Hurricane

131

In recent years I have volunteered at Duxford in the school holidays for "Meet the Veterans" and I was bitterly disappointed when they stopped doing that. I covered the Secret Army and made mock-ups from bits of tins and wood and things. Amongst these items were:

A Molotov Cocktail (people think it is just petrol, but it needs to be a mix of petrol, paraffin and crude oil which keeps it burning. Petrol makes one big whoosh and it's gone, almost no good at all.)

A rifle grenade launcher (as mentioned in Chapter 8).

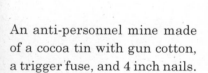

An anti-personnel mine made of a cocoa tin with gun cotton, a trigger fuse, and 4 inch nails.

A biscuit tin anti-tank mine which had nails with no heads, and a 22 round with bullet removed on either end. There are also fakes, made visible by being poorly hidden to make the enemy try to go round, and run over hidden ones on their diversion!

In Ransomes workshops I had six special daggers made up for the patrol. You go up behind the victim, slice their throat with one end and stab them with the other. I only have a wooden replica now.

Then there was the "carpet-sweeper" pill box destroyer. Gun cotton came in 3" x 2" x 6" blocks. We would pack several of these inside a wooden frame with a handle, and a long fuse that burns at the rate of one foot per minute. That gave you three minutes to lean that up against the pill box and run away. We did this at Aldeburgh. You would think the device would simply blow away from the concrete wall but gun cotton goes against the greatest resistance and cracks the wall instead.

My device replicas are mentioned in John Warwicker's book "Churchill's Underground Army" on page 155.

Chapter 21
The ACA and lovely companions

Since my retirement from the railway I have been doing quite a number of jobs in my spare time such as decorating and keeping peoples gardens tidy. My hearing is not so good, as I am a bit deaf in some frequencies. This was less due to the Wellingtons and Lancasters than to the whistling of the big diesels, all those miles riding in the back cab of the double-ended D31 diesel engines.

I joined the Suffolk & District branch of the Aircrew Association when it was formed in the late 1970s and was our local treasurer for fourteen years or so when we had 147 members. We had some great get-togethers with ex-crew members who had served all over the world.

I knew Spitfire pilot John Osborne from Little Bromley in Essex, and gave him a picnic table to suit the old Rolls Royce he was restoring. John Peake from nearby Frating was a Seafire Pilot who used to come along with him. Whenever they arrived together I would say, "Here come the biscuit brothers!"

I used to dress up in different costumes, such as a country yokel, and tell humorous and saucy stories and jokes at the ACA parties and dinners.

After nearly thirty years we had to lay up our standard at St Clement Danes, the RAF Church in London, because of the small number of wartime members still alive. I said to the remainder of them "I have left £1,000 in my will so you can all have a drink and a party when I go. But all you buggers keep dying off before me, and when my time comes there will be only a handful of you to drink all that, so I have decided it would be best to do it early!" So, I have already held my own wake, when I was still alive aged 85! There were 76 of them came along and everyone had a gift.

Our ACA has closed as a branch but a dozen or so of us still go for a monthly lunch as we have known each other about 30 years. I have written several poems, some of them a bit too saucy for this book, but here follows one I wrote in appreciation of the Air Crew Association.

The ACA - what does it mean?

The ACA - what does it mean?
A club for lads who have flyers been.
Most were quite young when flying they did
When shillings were bobs and a pound - a quid!

They gather each month to reminisce,
to talk of that and then of this.
They flew by day and in the dark,
then back to base the planes to park.

When they came back they looked around
to see if friends were safe and sound.
But if they weren't they had to hope
they had bailed out, the rip-cord groped.

They thought of sisters and of brothers,
but most of all their wives and mothers.
And when the job they did was done
then into civvies for some fun!

But in those days the friendships found
were different from those on the ground.
Some that endure through all the years
through all the trials, the sweat, the tears.

So let us hope the Club survives -
at least until I am 105!
And as we all get old and frail,
we can still laugh and tell a tale.
So those in future ne'er forget
the lads who died. We owe a debt!

Master of Ceremonies for ACA celebration of the 50th Anniversary of VE Day

I was left on my own after losing Sally, but was lucky enough to find two wonderful companions through the ACA. ✿

The first was Joan, whose husband had been a mosquito night fighter pilot. After he died, I saw her once and asked why she didn't still come along, and she said she didn't like to on her own. I started giving her a lift and we became friendly, and after that I came to live with her for 12 years. The last three years she was sadly wheelchair bound, and suffering from Alzheimer's disease, so I did everything for her. I bought a campervan to suit the wheelchair and used it to drive her round. We always went to Fairford Royal International Air Tattoo (which I have attended for the last 27 years).

I hadn't realised she was relatively wealthy as her husband had become a director of Eastern County Farmers. When she died and the will was read, it said I could stay in her bungalow for as long as I like if I paid all the bills. Furthermore, if I have to go into a home, the property would be sold off by the estate to support me. I was quite shocked at this surprise generosity.

In 2005 I had a severe heart attack. It happened one morning just as I got out of bed, but luckily the phone was right at hand so I was able to ring 999 right away. ✿ The operator was marvellous and had some paramedics with me in about five minutes. Then the ambulance arrived and I was taken to Ipswich hospital where I stayed for a week in intensive care. I was told to take things very easy for a few months. After a check-up I was able to lead a normal life, providing I take things relatively gently and keep taking the prescribed pills.

In 2007 I had another set-back, when I was told that I had sugar diabetes. I had to take even more pills and try to keep off eating anything sweet and not have sugar in my tea, which was a real shock to my system after all those years!

Parade Marshall

A Project Propeller trip

My companion now is Joy, whose husband was a WOp/AG same as me. I knew them for years, but her husband died about the same time as Sally. We get on so well together and have so much in common it is a great pleasure to spend time with her. I live at hers and sleep at mine. She cooks my meals and I do her garden. We act like a couple of recycled teenagers at times, and long may it continue.

Joy and I, however, do have two little words that are a darned nuisance to us both: O-L-D and A-G-E!

I am not religious, so I registered myself at Cambridge University so they can have my body for whatever they want. A woman once told me, "My husband appreciated no end the first person he dissected – the body had been donated and he was able to cut and learn a lot with no fear of hurting."

I don't know whether they will use any of my organs. Everything is worn out by now – especially the best bits! When I go to the Gents I say to the young fellows, "This is the best thing you can have when you are young, but when you get over 90 it's a bloody nuisance!"

Great-grandfather Potter, the blacksmith at Baylham, had an old British-made tobacco jar which he kept and handed down to me, and I in turn have handed the jar to my nephew James to carry on in the family.

The words written on it have become the Potter family motto:

Never say die. Up man, and try!

Epilogue
The End?

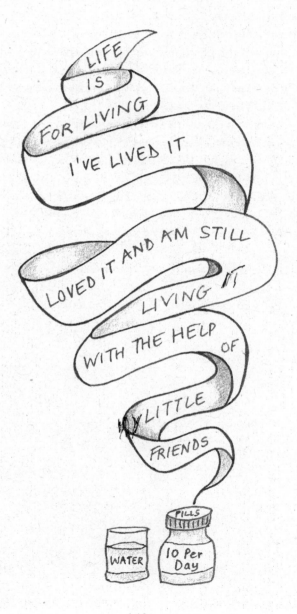

Illustration by my great-granddaughter Enya

Author's acknowledgements

I was a little anxious that this book might be confused with my first, considering the similar background of Ivan Potter with Peter Potter (farming, Home Guard and Secret Army, RAF service on Lancaster bombers) and even the same surname, although no relation. If anyone is concerned it may be the same book in a new cover, then rest assured that the content is quite different within!

I want to thank Ivan for entrusting me with his book. The tales have gradually sucked me into the Potter family and Suffolk ways in fascinating fashion over the weeks we worked on it. I also want to sincerely thank his two brothers, Stan and Mick, who are both tremendous characters in their own right.

My thanks go to Ann Strange for assistance and support; my sister Dorothy O'Grady for more fine maps and illustrations; Niels Reynolds and Rory O'Brine for help with the cover design, and to my eagle-eyed proof readers.

I appreciate how John and all the staff at CZ Design and Print have cheerfully made the production process quite effortless.

I hope you enjoy this story and chuckle as much as I did in the making of it. I dedicate this work to my ever-supportive mother, Jillian Mary Frostick.

Hugh Gunter Frostick
October 2017

"Tales of Peter Potter"
by Hugh Frostick

ISBN 9780995793804
Frostick Publishing

Available online from
www.frostick.co.uk

As recommended by
Air Marshall Sir Freddie Sowrey, KCB, CBE, AFC

Peter Louis Potter shares his eventful life from "clodhopper to cloud-topper and fire-stopper". His revealing and sometimes risqué tales range from Essex farming and village life, wartime service on Lancaster bombers, working in a mental asylum, and as a fireman in Colchester. Never short of an idea for a laugh or an adventure, and often bending the rules, Peter gives a wonderful feel for how he and his family lived and worked at Fobbing on the Essex marshes and the industrialised Thames, and farming near Colchester at Easthorpe, Fingringhoe and Mersea Island.

When war came, Peter ran away from home to volunteer for RAF Bomber Command, leading to many exciting episodes in Churchill's Secret Army and as a Lancaster rear gunner. Peter's skill as a raconteur has been well captured by Hugh Frostick in this highly entertaining account that gives a fascinating insight into life and war in the 20th Century.

Your book next?

Frostick Publishing can produce your own story for you. We specialise in bringing your tales to life, with skilful editing to ensure the reader does not become bored with minute detail. We are also expert in drawing out tales from older subjects, and with clever questioning can fill the gaps to make the story flow. We dislike disjointed reading material ourselves, so we always strive to create easy reading.

Alternatively, we can help you to print and publish a book you have written yourself.

Services include:

- Introductory chat to give opinion on your story
- Interviewing and recording subject and associated persons
- Transcribing recordings (ours or yours)
- Scanning and enhancing photographs
- Limited historical research
- Producing maps and artwork
- Editing and proofreading
- Book layout (typesetting) and cover design
- Registering ISBN book number
- Providing proof copy and instructing printer
- Marketing and despatch by separate arrangement

Pricing:

Interviewing, writing and editing cost is £25 per hour. Artwork cost is £50 per hour. A travel rate will be negotiated per trip according to location. If you are far from Essex, we will consider travelling to stay with you or near you to capture the information, at your expense.

Example book estimates (from scratch):

Tales of Peter Potter (300 pages)	£3,500-£4,500
Mister Lucky by Ivan Potter (150 pages)	£2,500-£3,000
Birthday Biography with family history	from £ 750

Note: softback book printing costs are extra, usually £2 to £3 per copy

More info about Frostick Publishing at www.frostick.co.uk